# HIGH ALTITUDE PLANTING

A practical guide to landscaping,
gardening, and planting above 6,000 feet.

How to. . .

What to. . .

When to. . .

Why bother?

by Ann Barrett

Published by Barrett Enterprises
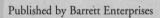

ISBN  0-9673331-0-5

Book designed by C&S Creative Services, Park City, UT

Printed in the U.S.A.

# ACKNOWLEDGEMENTS

When you talk about something for a long time, (YEARS), and, finally, one day, you just sit down and write it. . . it seems like you owe everyone an apology for making them wait so long.

So, all of you living above 6,000' elevation or wallowing in a cold pocket, I'm sorry.
*We're* sorry.

We, because a project like this is not me; it is a culmination of asking, answering, asking and repeating the answers to all kinds of questions that have popped up in the last 17 years. It is the group effort of all my colleagues: my husband Steve, Jeanne, Russ, Dana, Kevin, John, Jackie, Laura, Susan, Barb, Leanne, Clara - wondering WHY things are so different up here. It is the extended resources of knowledgeable people in various fields: Steve, Lon and Donna, Tad and Sheila, Dave, Lyn and Melody, Henry, Russ, Kevin, Janet, Lori, Todd, Cathy, Skip, Amy and Dave; and our family support team: the Kermizises and the Barretts.

It is "hands on" experience that finds its way into our memory banks and keeps our lungs full of fresh air and our fingernails dirty.

To Creative Landscaping above 6,000'.<br>Work from the ground up. . .

I

# TABLE of CONTENTS

## Chapter II: WHAT TO. ...  31

# Introduction

Being "Nursery People" at above 6,500' elevation over the past 17 years, we have had a unique opportunity to make many observations and evaluations of HIGH ALTITUDE GARDENING.

We hope that you will find this book interesting or at least helpful so that you may avoid some of our mistakes and make progress toward new ideas of your own.

The first rule is that NOTHING is as it seems. Just because a plant is labeled Zone 2 (theoretically hardy) does not mean it will flourish at altitude - likewise, a Zone 4 plant may do great "up here" even though it is not zoned as capable. The reason: an extremely short growing season. All the varieties you choose for your yard need to be able to "do their thing" in about two months. BUD, BLOOM, FOLIATE, FALL COLOR, DE-FOLIATE and be dormant through our late spring!  Sounds impossible, but there are many varieties of trees, shrubs, perennials, bi-annuals that produce master gardener and cottage garden beauty above 6,500'.

Follow our lead. . .Gardening is a matter of opinion and we are all entitled to our own. Drive around, learn what you like and don't like, get an idea for yourself - it is going to be your living space. Keep in the front of your mind, though, that you live in the high desert mountains. You may have to adjust some of your preferences to accommodate the elevation.

# chapter 1: HOW TO. . .

*"All life is an experiment.*
*The more experiments you make, the better."*
-Ralph Waldo Emerson

# PLAN and DESIGN YOUR GARDEN, YARD and LIVING SPACE

Determine how you want to play in your yard. Draw a sketch showing where your house sits on your property. (This sketch need only be as detailed as your imagination requires - some of us need 'to scale' drawings, others can go off a rough sketch)
Include:

  Play areas and manicured areas

  Gardening areas

  Perennial/Bedding areas

  Wild to open space - if construction left you some
        natural, indigenous vegetation, don't mess with it. . .
        maybe irrigate and add to it.

Examine your exposures:
  Sunny areas
  Morning sun, afternoon shade
  Afternoon sun, morning shade
  Deep shade areas
  Future shade areas

Windy......
  all day
  protected from the wind
  occasional wind

## DESIGN AN EFFICIENT SPRINKLER SYSTEM:

Design a sprinkler system or have it designed to complement your area. Use water efficiently. Shrub heads in shrub areas, spray, stream rotors or impact heads for lawns, drip irrigation in windy areas and around trees - and wherever else it is feasible. Proper heads adjusted properly are important. Do your homework. Water is a valuable resource and there is no need to waste it with all the technology available.

## PREPARE A PLANTING AREA:

No matter where you live and grow, SOIL is the single most important key to success. As a rule, mountain climate soil is very rocky, clay-like, and alkaline. The tricks to creating a good growing medium are soil amendments and additional topsoil.

Our favorite amendments are as follows:

1) MULCH or SOIL PEP® ( a fir and cedar by-product) it helps break up the clay, creates a better growing medium and aids with soil drainage.
2) GYPSUM is a mineral that breaks down clay and replaces alkali salts (helps aerate the soil).
   It only needs to be broadcast a couple of times (heavily) during the life-cycle of your yard. It can be used more frequently if it is broadcast lighter than recommended.

> GYPSUM TIP:
> It is helpful to spread gypsum in the fall by areas close to winter salt, like beds along roads and near salted paths.

3) COMPOST- preferably a Live Compost - adds live organic matter to our lack-luster soil - Very Important!

4) SOIL SULFUR and SOIL ACIDIFIER help lower the pH of the soil. The closer to neutral your soil can be, the better most plants will grow. Our water is also frequently alkaline, which doesn't help.

$$- \quad \text{IDEAL} \quad +$$

-7 ——————— 0 ——————— +7

Acidic        Neutral        Alkaline

*pH Diagram*

Soil amendments can be used in entire planting areas or individually on trees and shrubs. (See How to Plant a Tree on page 8)

After determining where you want to create perennial beds, attempt vegetable gardens, plant wildflower seed, create shade, etc., it is essential to eliminate ALL undesirable vegetation. This can be accomplished through chemical weed control, . . . (i.e.: several applications of a non-selective weed killer in conjunction with tilling or, repeated tilling and a lot of weeding). It is not an option - all unwanted vegetation must be removed from the root-up. A broken off root will continue to grow. . . if only everything grew so easily!

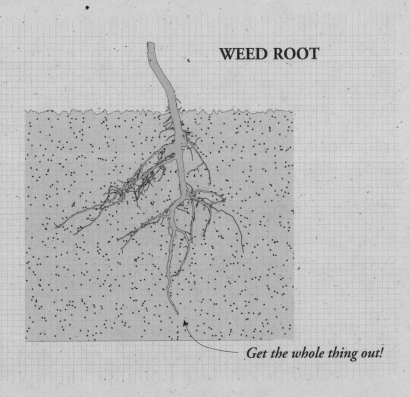

## WEED ROOT

*Get the whole thing out!*

Round-up® and other non-selective weed killers neutralize when they touch bare dirt. They only work on actively growing vegetation. They are taken in through the leaves, processed by the plant and kill from the root up. It takes about two weeks of 65 degree temperatures or better.

When you are satisfied with your weed kill and soil texture, can you go out and dig with a trowel instead of a pic-axe? If you can, then you are ready for planting. Proper weed extermination and soil preparation can take several weeks, maybe even months. DON'T SKIMP ON THIS STEP!

## How to: CREATE a BERM

Berming up low or flat areas is a relatively common way to add dimension to your yard. It is also a good way to plant areas with high water tables.

By bringing in topsoil and adding soil amendments you can add height to screen and block areas instantly, as well as ensure a good planting medium for your immediate root system establishment.

When creating berms, GENTLY slope them to just above knee level. Try not to make them too steep or water will run off too quickly and not be absorbed by the plants.

## TO CREATE A NEW PLANTING AREA

1) Take a garden hose or string marker and outline the area. Try several shapes. . .

2) When you like the shape, use a non-selective herbicide like Killzall®
   or Round-Up® to kill the grass.

3) When the grass has begun to die off - about 1½ - 2 weeks, you can turn it
   over with a shovel or roto-till it to break up the root mass.

4) Add fresh soil mixture to area.

5) Leave a 1' strip around the border unplanted since grass is very aggressive and may
   encroach into the bed - particularly along the edges where soil is less than 6" deep.

## How to: PLANT TREES PROPERLY

Use care when handling your plants. Remember, you are dealing with living things - DON'T DROP THEM!

If your ground is super hard, (undiggable), start your hole with a pick and shovel, fill it with water, let the water drain (½ hour or so). The moisture will soften the soil. Remove the soft soil and repeat as necessary.

> ### TREE WELLS:
> Maintaining the integrity of your tree well by keeping it weed and grass free will always ensure a healthier tree or shrub - less competition for water and less likely to be "weed whacked" on lawn maintenance day. Weed eaters are one of the leading causes of injury and death to established plants.

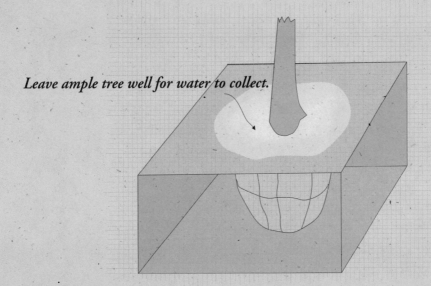

*Leave ample tree well for water to collect.*

# HOW to PLANT A BALLED and BURLAPPED TREE

1) Dig a hole 6-12" larger than the pot or rootball.

2) Add mulch and live compost to the soil
   you dig out. 50/50 mix of topsoil and mulch mix.

3) Fill bottom of the hole 6-12" with the mixture.

4) Gently place the plant in the hole STRAIGHT.

5) Backfill ⅓ of rootball, tamp soil and continue to backfill another ⅓.
   Make sure there are no air pockets around the rootball or under it.
   Finish filling hole.

6) Leave a nice well around the plant to collect water.

7) Water thoroughly - allow soil to dry between watering. DO NOT
   let the roots dry out completely or stay soaked.

8) Fertilize with a root stimulant at time of planting and 3-4 times
   throughout the growing season. Fertilize every 4-6 weeks for the first 2
   seasons with Morgro®Rootstarter.

9) Water requirements will vary throughout the season depending on
   the air temperature and seasonal moisture. Dig a small test hole
   3-5" below the surface and check. If the soil is relatively damp,
   wait a day or more to water. If it is dry, water and check again the next day.

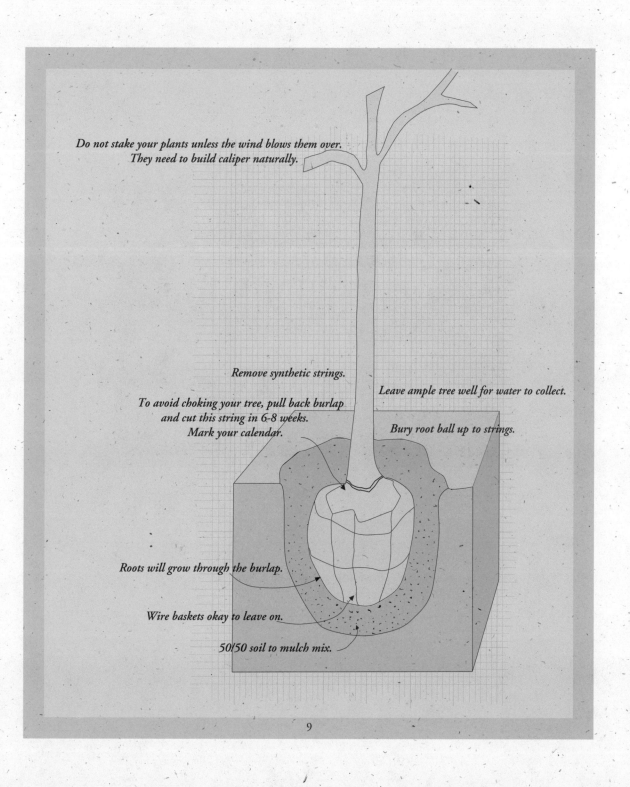

Do not stake your plants unless the wind blows them over.
They need to build caliper naturally.

Remove synthetic strings.

Leave ample tree well for water to collect.

To avoid choking your tree, pull back burlap
and cut this string in 6-8 weeks.
Mark your calendar.

Bury root ball up to strings.

Roots will grow through the burlap.

Wire baskets okay to leave on.

50/50 soil to mulch mix.

**HARDSCAPING:**
Using benches, chairs, arbors, birdbaths and feeders, stepping stones, etc., is a perfect way to go from a visual space to an interaction area.

## How to:  PLANT SHRUBS PROPERLY

- ✿ Balled and Burlapped (B&B) shrubs - See "How to Plant A Tree" page 8
- ✿ Potted Shrubs:

1) Dig hole 5-12" larger than the pot, add soil mixture to bottom of
   hole (Mulch, Compost, Gypsum, Topsoil).

2) Gently remove plant from the pot WITHOUT disturbing the root mass.
   If the roots are "pot bound" or very dense, it may be necessary to break them
   up a little bit with a knife or shovel.

3) Place in hole - straight

4) Backfill with soil mix - tamping constantly to make sure there are no air
   pockets.

5) Fertilize and check watering the same as B&B above.

✿ Bare-root anything is not advised.  Due to the extremely short growing season and large game population, these youngsters don't have much of a chance. It is better to purchase plants with established root systems. We're not saying you can't do it but. . . a bare root plant will be behind its established counterpart 3-5 years - IF it survives. (This was one of our earliest, lengthiest, and costliest mistakes.  We tried to "root out" bare root shrubs for over seven years - planting them in the spring, irrigating them all summer, losing more than ½ the crop by the following spring, and still barely having a rooted plant by the end of the second growing season.  OH WELL. . . )

## How to: PLANT FLOWERS

❋ From starts: Hopefully you have prepared an easy-to-dig, enjoyable planting medium. At this point, all you have to do is: (1) dig a hole at least as large as the container you have purchased: rose-pot, 4", 5", gallon, 5-gallon container, etc.

2) Take the plant out of the container and remove a small portion of the root mass. This allows the plant to root out quicker.

3) Plant very firmly in the soil-mix so that when you tug gently on the foliage, it doesn't pop out of the soil.

4) Water in with a mild fertilizer like Morgro®Rootstarter or ferti-lome® Blooming and Rooting Formula. Try not to over water, but do not let the plants get bone dry. Always check with your finger or a moisture meter.

5) Don't expect a great show the first season. Just try to get the roots established and some notable top growth. It takes about 3 years to really fill in, depending on how closely you plant your starts. 6" - 12" - 18" - 2' apart is our general rule, depending on the variety.

## How to: PLANT WILDFLOWER SEED

Prepare the soil according to the size of the proposed seed area and your budget. Try to use Gypsum and Morgro® Sod & Seed Starter fertilizer to start. Soil Pep® and new topsoil over massive areas can be quite costly but the more you can add to an area, the better foundation your wildflower patch will have.

1) Eliminate existing weeds and unwanted vegetation.

2) Amend the soil to increase germination success.

3) Using a rake, loosen the soil to create small furrows for the seed to lie in after it is broadcast.

4) Broadcast seed by hand or with a spreader for a more even distribution. Use coverage estimates recommended on the tag. It is almost humanly impossible to cover more than 2,000 square feet with 1 pound of seed.

5) Water gently and thoroughly 2-3 times daily until it germinates. Germination occurs in 2-8 weeks depending on the temperature and when the seed is sown.

> The combination of heat and water make seed germinate. If spring and summer temperatures are low, it WILL take longer to germinate.
>
> PATIENCE, PATIENCE, PATIENCE...

6) Continue watering daily. DO NOT overwater or underwater. After seed germinates, watering schedule can be reduced to every-other-day and eventually even less frequently.

7) By eliminating weeds throughout summer and fall during the growing season, you will create a healthier environment for your seed to flourish - more space for flowers, less space for unwanted plant material.

Wildflower seed blends, like Park City Nursery's Original Custom Wildflower Blends®, with a balanced mixture of ¾ perennials, ¼ annuals, should bloom the first season if sown before mid-June or July.

It requires a patient planter to wait for nature to work its miracles

*Wildflower planting without soil amendments.*

*Wildflower planting with soil amendments*

## How to: PLAN and PLANT CONTAINER GARDENS

Planting in containers is an excellent way to experience summer. They are useful in small spaces, add color and are easy to bring inside in case of frost. Just looking at them will make you happy.

TYPES OF CONTAINERS YOU MAY USE: Remember, they need to be large enough to handle some root growth and they need good drainage.

- plastic
- wooden
- Italian terra-cotta**
- baskets
- barrels
- buckets
- Mexican terra-cotta**
- crates
- ANY PLANT HOLDER YOU CAN DREAM UP!

**terra-cotta tends to wick moisture away from the soil. Try using some of the water storing gels and crystals now on the market.

**Soil**: Always use fresh potting soil. Be careful to avoid cheap, porous, sandy soil. Good potting soil has a certain feel; it can absorb moisture and drain properly.

## WHAT PLANTS TO CHOOSE:

- Trees and Shrubs: Aspen, Spruce, Juniper, Dwarf Alberta Spruce, small ornamentals, Siberian pea shrub, Lilac, etc. Container must be large enough to accommodate the root mass. Don't expect them to live very long in the pot. They stand a pretty good chance of dying over the winter, if not the first season, then the second or third year.

- Flowers: Hardy annuals like Snapdragons, Pansy, Viola, Petunia, Dracena (spikes),

- Asparagus fern, Dianthus, Geranium, Lobelia, "Proven Winners," Gaura, etc.

- Herbs: Any you can find that you enjoy or that look and smell good- "medicinal remedy pot," "cooking," "tea," "ornamental."

- Vegetables: Salads are fun - gourmet lettuces, radishes, onions, chives, cucumbers, tomatoes, peppers, etc.

- Perennials: Usually don't bloom long enough but can be transplanted back into the yard when they are done. Try assorted groundcovers, Hens and Chicks, Roses, Asters, Carnations, Dianthus, Silver Brocade, etc.

- Bulbs: Narcissus, Daffodils, Crocus, Tulips, Allium, Windflowers, Dutch Iris, etc.

**Planting:** Think about where you will be placing your containers and design them accordingly. Since the growing season is so short, stuff your planters full of flowers. No time to wait for the pots to fill in on their own!

1) Tallest varieties in back, graduating down to trailing varieties

2) "Bulls-eye" - tallest varieties in center, moving down to trailing borders.

Symmetry in a container can be achieved by:
     "Twinning" - matching sides identically
     "Complementing" - choosing plants with different textures but similar colors and matching sides with complementary color schemes.

**Water**: Usually daily depending on the soil and the amount of sun and wind.

**Fertilize:** Frequently - every week or so, with a blooming mix or fish emulsion, or try the new polymers on the market with slow release fertilizers.

## How to: CARE FOR NEWLY PLANTED PLANTS

**FERTILIZING:** Use Morgro® Rootstarter or some type of root stimulant every 4-6 weeks throughout the first 1½-2 growing seasons. The object is to get well established, healthy roots the first season. Top growth and flowers are not important at this point, merely bonuses!

**WATERING:** Overwatering (surprisingly) is the most dominant mistake new plant owners make, followed by not watering frequently enough. There is no exact formula for watering. Everyone has different soil-moisture retention and every year claims different spring, summer, fall, and winter precipitation. As the caretaker, you need to be in touch with nature. If it is raining a significant amount, turn your sprinkler off. If the area is experiencing a drought, efficient supplemental watering may be necessary.

WARNING:
Overwatering kills Spruce. Spruce need to DRY OUT between waterings.
How Much Water? Thoroughly soak root ball and wait 5 days. Then dig down next to root ball to determine dampness. Continue checking every day until root ball is somewhat dry. Soak Again.

RULES of THUMB for PLANTING:
If you dig a hole, and there is water in the hole, DO NOT PLANT.
If you dig a hole, and the soil removed from the hole is mucky, DO NOT PLANT.
If either of the above conditions exist, plant in raised bed or berm. (see page 6)

WHAT IF you have a SPRINKLER SYSTEM?
Sprinklers are designed to water lawn. It can either be too much or not enough water. Check your root ball regularly.

REMEMBER: Spruce are not the only tree that can be killed by overwatering.

## How to: CARE FOR ESTABLISHED PLANTS

FERTILIZING: A healthy plant can withstand many of nature's woes: drought, pestilence, etc. An annual fertilizing schedule for your trees, shrubs and flowers will help. Spring, summer and/or fall is sufficient. Do not over use fertilizer. It can interfere with the natural process of micro-organisms exchanging nutrients between the soil and the roots. Too much fertilizer replaces the job of the micro-organisms, causing them to die and leaving a dead soil. Use a well-rounded formula like: **16* 16* 8, 16* 16* 16, 10*10*10.**

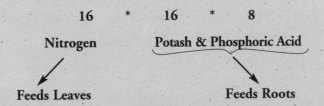

**16 * 16 * 8**

**Nitrogen**      **Potash & Phosphoric Acid**

**Feeds Leaves**      **Feeds Roots**

WATERING: Again, it is impossible to say every other day, every third day, once a week (DEFINITELY not every day). It all depends on our natural precipitation and monthly rainfall, your soil's moisture retention capability. The old finger, moisture meter or shovel next to the drip line will tell all.

It is far better to water less frequently and deeper than daily with less. Daily watering promotes shallow root growth and this does not benefit plants in a high mountain desert. Deep roots are better - they create sturdier plants more capable of retrieving available water from the ground.

How to: IDENTIFY PROBLEMS

Overwatering:  Yellowing leaves, upturned leaves, soggy soil, fungus on the leaves or trunk.

Underwatering:  Yellowing leaves, droopy leaves, dry cracks in the soil surrounding the plant, moisture meter registers "Dry".

Insects:  One advantage to high elevation gardening is that there are relatively few horrible bugs. We mainly have to deal with Aphids, Leaf Miners, some Slugs, White Pine Weevil, Spruce Gall, some Tent-worm, and a few miscellaneous seasonal problems.

Porcupine Damage:  Chewed area around the trunks of Pines, Firs, Crabapples, and anything else that appeals to them, especially soft barked trees - USE repellents or traps to relocate them. Sometimes wrapping the trunk of the tree with a trunk protector will discourage them.

Big Game:  Can be as minor as "munched" new buds to crushed limbs. -USE repellents to dissuade them. Dogs may help a little.

# How to: USE CHEMICALS FOR PREVENTATIVE and CURATIVE TASKS
### Always, always, always follow the instructions on the labels!

Chemicals come in several basic categories - there are organic alternatives:

- Insecticides - kill insects which can cause severe damage and even death, different types are specific to different pests.
- Dormant Oil - spray oil which can be applied to deciduous plants before they leaf out. It suffocates any eggs or larvae on the plant. Do not use on Evergreens.
- Lady Bugs - an organic alternative to insecticides; they attack and kill aphids and other undesirable insects on plants.
- Fungicides - help control and prevent airborne and ground fungus.
- Fertilizers - provide nutrients to plants.
- Herbicides - kill grasses and plants which can be a nuisance in your yard - <u>Non-Selective Weed Killers</u> - kill any growing thing they touch; <u>Selective Weed Killers</u> - kill either narrow leaf or broadleaf plants; <u>Pre-Emergents</u> -hinder the growth of seeds before they break the ground surface.
- Baits - lure pests to them, are ingested by the pest and kills them.
- Repellents - keep animals away from areas they have been applied.

---

TIP: When spraying herbicides, add Soil Acidifier and Spreader Sticker to your chemical. This little cocktail will make your application more effective.

---

When dealing with nature there are, at times, undesirable conditions which need to be confronted. Again, always double-check the label.

How to: DEAL WITH SPECIFIC PROBLEMS:

**Boring Insects:** Leave holes in bark. USE: Lindane, Dursban, Sevin®

**Aphids:** Minuscule, profuse insects that can suck the life out of leaves and branches.
USE: Dursban, Diazinon, Thiodan®.

**Spruce Gall:** An aphid that lays its eggs in the tender new growth tips of Spruce trees. After they hatch, they eat their way out of the tree, exiting via the holes they have made, leaving a hard, cone-like encasement where the new growth would have been. USE: Thiodan® as soon as the tree breaks bud.

**Black Spot** on Aspen: Black spots all over Aspen leaves. Usually the result of too much direct moisture on the leaves. Not detrimental unless it occurs several years in a row, chronically. USE: Daconil® as a preventative when the trees first leaf out in conjunction with an insecticide. (So you only have to spray once, maybe twice.)

**Cytospora:** An airborne fungus that usually attacks Aspen - recognized by raised black spots on trunk and tell-tale pinkish/orange bark. Use a strong Systemic Fungicide. If that doesn't cure it, dispose of the plant before it can infect any other trees - Highly contagious.

**Voles, Moles, Field Mice:** Come from outer lying meadows - mostly in the winter, under the snow. They burrow through the lawn, eating grass roots and tunneling around, often devastating the lawn. You may try to prevent this by using a Fungicide/Repellent in the fall: Thiram®, Terrachlor® or maybe even Milorganite®. Smoke bombs and Baits may work when you know where they are in a given area.

**Grass in your ground cover and flowers:** Selective weed killers that identify and kill grass and NOT broad leaves: Poast®, Over-the-Top®.

**Dandelions and Clover in your lawn:** Selective weed killers that kill broad leaves and NOT grass: Morgro® Weed-it-II with Trimec®.

**Open soil:** in newly planted flower beds ideal for weed seeds to germinate. USE: Pre-emergent granules or liquid. Usually contain Treflan®, Triamine®, or Caseron®.

**Tent worm:** Recognized by its webbed appearance among the branches of trees and shrubs. USE: Thuricide®, Diazinon, Dursban.

**White Pine Weevil/Tip Weevil:** USE: Lindane, Dursban, Sevin (see following article).

## A BIG PROBLEM with a "NO-OPTION" SOLUTION

Have you ever noticed Spruce turning brown on top and apparently dying from the top-down?

Identifying the Problem: The problem is the White Pine Weevil (*pissodes strobi),* nicknamed "tip-weevil". It attacks the leader or terminal shoot of Spruce trees from about 8-30 years old - rarely younger, but it is most severe on evenly spread trees of approximately the same age.

The first sign of damage is small, boring holes in the bark on the leaders of healthy trees. Both feeding and laying eggs cause holes that exude pitch. Later in the season, the tree appears to be dying from the top-down.

Life Cycle of the White Pine Weevil:  In April, May and June, adult weevils make feeding punctures on terminal growth of the preceding year. They crawl up the tree on the warm days of early spring to feed on wood or buds. Then they mate.

In May and June, they lay between 50 and 150 eggs in the terminals. Upon hatching, yellowish grubs group together in bands. The developing larvae girdle and kill the terminals but NOT until the new growth has elongated. It is easy to spot the wilted, bent, infested terminals at this time. The needles on the secondary growth turn reddish and fall off also.

The larvae move downward as they mature, emerging as adult beetles in late summer where they continue to feed on bud and bark tissue. They overwinter in forest litter, in the ground. Other portions of the "hatch" or "brood" overwinter as larvae and pupae in the infested terminals. Although there is only one generation per year, there is considerable overlapping of broods.

Prevention:  Spray spruce tips as they bud out or a couple of weeks before  (at elevation this is usually late May-early June) with Dursban, Lindane or Sevin® - insecticides for boring insects. Then as your spruce begin to die-back in late June and early July, cut the top out 3-6" below the infected area and dispose of as advised.

The Cure: Cut off the infected tips well into the healthy, non-affected area to ensure complete containment of the weevil. It is essential to cut deep enough into the good wood as they may be much deeper than the symptoms indicate.

The best disposal is to burn the clippings. Fire districts have specific burn permits for residential yard maintenance. Call yours.

If you live in an area where burning is prohibited, like within the city limits, or you are cutting during a non-burn period, you can enclose the infected branches in a plastic bag. This should suffocate the insects, plus once they run out of nutrients, they should die.

To avoid multiple tops after you have cut the top out of your tree, you need to "train" a new leader. This is accomplished by choosing a strong branch near the center of the tree and affixing it to a stake. After one growing season, remove the stake.

It's your yard, they're your trees, this is a serious situation which can be cured with community cooperation. If everyone checked for *pissodes strobi*, (White Pine Weevil) this year and cut it out of their own trees, the epidemic would lessen annually, and Spruce would start to shape up nicely!

## How to:  MAYBE KEEP DEER AWAY?

Keeping deer and other desirable, but not always welcome, animals away from your plants, is an ongoing struggle. Here are some suggestions:

## ORGANIC SOLUTIONS:

- Lifeboy soap lathered onto the foliage
- Home Brew:  1 quart water/ 1 egg/ 1 tsp. Szechuan hot oil.
    Put in blender until well mixed. Put in sprayer and mist once a week
    and after rain - supposedly deer hate the smell of rotting eggs.

## OTHER METHODS:

- Electric fencing around your property
- Fencing off tender new shoots and young plants
- Repellents:  Ro-Pel®, This-1-Works®, Deer Away® - available at nurseries and
    garden centers.

    Apply once in late fall, once in spring, and throughout the season as needed.

PLANTS DEER LIKE LESS: (porcupines are another story. . .)

<u>Annuals:</u> Marigold, Petunia, Herbs, Godetia, Wallflower, Viola. . .

<u>Perennials:</u> Snow-in-Summer, Fleabane, Cranesbill Geranium, Gaillardia, Lamium, Daylily, Daffodils, Daisy, Foxglove, Meadowsage, Iris, Stratford Blue Salvia, Narcissus, Creeping Phlox, Potentilla Verna, Nepeta, Penstemon, Purple and Prairie Coneflowers, Sedum, Thyme, Saint Johnswort, Yarrow, Centaurea, Armeria, Silver Mound, Crocus, Ajuga, Fragaria, Coreopsis, Scabiosa, Lambs Ear, assorted Mints. . .

<u>Shrubs and Trees:</u>  Juniper, Lilac, Siberian Peashrub, Spruce, Scrub Oak, Barberry, Cotoneaster, Gooseberry, Sumac.

PLANTS THEY ADORE: (tender new growth on just about anything!)
Flanders Poppy, Flowering Crabapple, Pine and Fir Trees, Tulips, Roses-most varieties, Scarlet Dropmore Honeysuckle Vine, Snapdragons, Spirea. . .

There can be <u>No Guarantees</u> on any of this information. A lean animal will eat what it must to survive. An undetected garden will fare fine. They were here first and we need to figure out a way to co-exist.

## How to: CHOOSE A FERTILIZER

A word about Chemical Fertilizers: They are usually less expensive than their organic counterparts. If you do not live near water where run-off is an issue, a balanced, granular chemical fertilizer will achieve acceptable results (16*16*8, 10*10*10).

Liquid chemical fertilizers and pure Nitrogen granular fertilizers leach out too fast and only provide a quick fix for your lawn, not a turf-building process. At this altitude, with our short summers and marginal soil, it is essential to fertilize seasonally and properly. An occasional high-Nitrogen dose is okay, but don't make a steady diet of it.

Organic Lawn Care: Is your only option if you live near a river, creek or lake. They do not leach as much as chemical fertilizers and are therefore safer to use near water to avoid algae accumulation and contamination.

Organic products also help microorganisms in the soil which keep your soil healthy and alive. They release considerably slower than most chemical fertilizers which provide a slower growing, longer-greening of the grass. You won't have to mow as often.

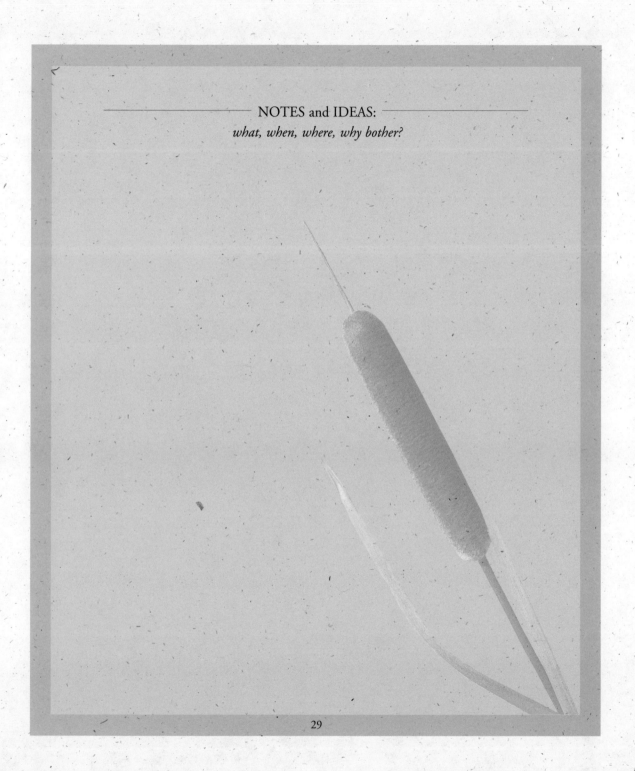

## chapter II: WHAT TO. . .

*"There is no guarantee on life. . ."*

*"I like trees because they seem more resigned*
*to the way they have to live than other things do."*
Willa Cather 1913

chapter II: WHAT TO. . .

Plant selection at elevation is different than anywhere else on earth. Due to the extremely short growing season, (we cannot stress this single factor enough), even more than extreme temperatures, choices are comparatively stream-lined (limited). You will find, though, that due to the cool summer temperatures, perennial gardens can be spectacular, much showier throughout the season than our hotter neighbors.

Elevation gardeners are disadvantaged due to general lack of experience and knowledge of high elevation planting. There are very few ACCURATE reference books or guides written to accommodate our needs. Many plants will survive in our environment but. . . FLOURISH is the word we want to subscribe to.

Within every community there are micro-climates. Each of these areas have unique needs and special considerations. In our area we can divide the community into Naturally Protected Areas, Sagebrush Country, Alpine Desert Regions, Alpine, Meadow and Plains Areas, Special Consideration Areas.

# BREAKDOWN OF MICROCLIMATES:

NATURALLY PROTECTED AREAS: Nestled in the foothills of the mountains with protection from constant wind and temperature fluctuations of more open areas. These areas are usually blessed with fairly decent soil, needing only minimal amendments. These areas were probably settled first and have large, established trees and shrubs as well as more homes closer together. These things provide protection from the elements which allows the gardener a larger plant pallet.

SAGEBRUSH COUNTRY: Harsh, high desert with the main, pre-existing vegetation of Sagebrush, Juniper and drought-tolerant wildflowers and grasses. Usually minimal to no protection from prevailing wind. Soil is generally lacking in nutrients and somewhat rocky. Deer, moose and elk roam freely.

ALPINE DESERT REGIONS: Slightly higher elevation. Pre-existing vegetation includes Aspen, Scrub Oak, Woods Rose, Serviceberry, Chokecherry, many native wildflowers and grasses. You may find varying soil conditions from rocky to loamy.

ALPINE: Elevations above 7,000'. Existing vegetation includes Alpine Fir, White Fir, Doug Fir, Aspen, Mountain Mahogany. Very rocky and exposed. Winter lasts longer here than anywhere else and summer is shorter and cooler.

MEADOW and PLAINS AREAS:  Some wetlands, higher water table, higher potential density in development. Have some decent soil, a bit flat for garden interest - needs some "berming-up" to create texture in the landscape.  (See how to: CREATE a BERM page 6.)

AREAS WITH SPECIAL CONSIDERATIONS:  Many high elevation communities were established because of mining. A by-product of mining, the tailings, are extremely toxic - frequently in the old days, these tailings were deposited down stream from the mining site. As a result of growth, people (us) today have to deal with this according to community standards. Fruit trees and veggies are out of the question. Try containerized gardening for your "edibles."

Micro-Climates within your own yard include:
- Protected sites near your home, especially eastern exposures.
- Fenced-in areas - living or structural.
- North Side - last section to lose snow pack.
- Exposed areas - windy areas.
- Particularly wet or dry areas.
- Native, indigenous areas - disturbed or undisturbed.
- Created areas of protection - tree and shrub placement as wind blocks and…
- partial shade for planting.

## WIND:

Wind is a nasty element. It greatly hinders plant growth. It is important to create wind barriers in your yard. This can be done with fences or by planting natural hedges of cold-hardy shrubs and trees along your prevailing windy borders.

We have found Siberian Pea Shrub, Serviceberry, Chokecherry, Aspen, Cottonwoods, Peking Cotoneaster, Arctic Blue Willow, Amur Maple, Lilac, Buffaloberry, and Canada Redcherry planted in groups, either mixed or by variety tend to create the most effective wind blocks.

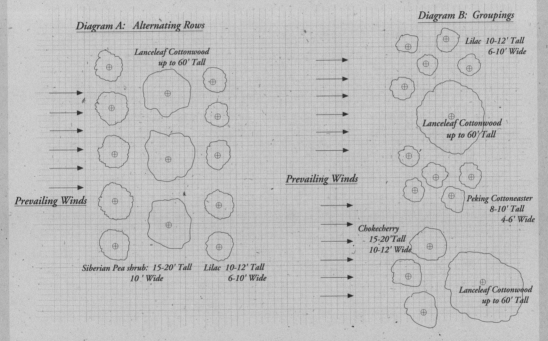

Diagram A: Alternating Rows

Lanceleaf Cottonwood up to 60' Tall

Prevailing Winds

Siberian Pea shrub: 15-20' Tall 10 ' Wide

Lilac 10-12' Tall 6-10' Wide

Diagram B: Groupings

Lilac 10-12' Tall 6-10' Wide

Lanceleaf Cottonwood up to 60' Tall

Prevailing Winds

Peking Cottoneaster 8-10' Tall 4-6' Wide

Chokecherry 15-20'Tall 10-12' Wide

Lanceleaf Cottonwood up to 60' Tall

Most shrubs and trees can be planted 6-15' apart. The closer you plant them, the quicker the screen will fill in. Once you have an effective wind barrier, you can plant more ornamental-type plants "inside" (Flowering Crabapple, Spruce, etc.).

Planting trees and shrubs in clusters is an excellent way to protect plants from the elements. The outer plants will break the wind so that the plants on the inside of the grouping will grow faster, bigger, better. . .

## CHOOSING THE RIGHT PLANT MATERIAL:

Not only do you need to choose plants that will grow in your area, but it is in your best interest to buy quality, seed-grown nursery stock from reputable outlets with suppliers from compatible growing locations.

TREES: Evergreen and Deciduous

Trees are an essential part of your landscape. They grow tall, provide shade, offer texture, take away the sharp angles of buildings, and increase the value of your property.

Creating shade in your yard helps conserve water of which we have limited supply in the high mountain desert. It helps cool your house in the summer and provides habitats for birds and other animals.
(See "Birdscaping" Plant List page 43)

A creative mix of evergreen and deciduous trees is pleasing to the eye. Groupings of these textures allow individual plants within the group to grow better. If you look around, plants that stand alone frequently suffer alone - give them some companions.

Following is a list of varieties which thrive at elevation when planted in the proper spot. There are many other varieties which grow here, but we want you to plant "winners." If you want to try something different, that is fine, good actually, but don't use your whole landscape as an experiment. Stick with predominantly tried and true. Countless varieties are zoned to our area but repeatedly come up short - winter kill/dieback; inability to leaf out and grow in the allotted growing season, or take more than three years to establish and flourish.

TRUST US. . .

We have put an asterisk next to your "Bread and Butter" varieties. Even when you plant established, quality grown nursery stock, it can take plants 3-5 years to get established and begin growing to their fullest potential. You are likely to lose an average of one out of every ten trees that you plant.

# EVERGREEN TREES

**Alpine Fir - Zone 2** *(Abies lasiocarpa)* Narrow, steeple-shaped evergreen to 50' tall; difficult to establish due to deep tap root, intermountain native. Bluish green needles. Shade-tolerant.

**Douglas Fir - Zone 2** *(Pseudotsuga menziesii)* Densely set, soft needles. Ends of branches swing up; does well in sun or shade; tolerates some wind. Grows to 60'; intermountain native.

**White Fir - Zone 3** *(Abies concolor)* Difficult to establish; prefers a nothern exposure; soft, bluish/white needles, conical shape.

**Austrian Pine - Zone 3** *(Pinus nigra)* Dark green needles 3-6½" long; grows to 40'; susceptible to winter burn and porcupine damage. Difficult to establish but hardy once established.

**\*Bristlecone Pine - Zone 2** *(Pinus aristata)* Extremely hardy, slow-growing to 20-45'. Unique, contorted habit and white resin on dark needles.

**Lodgepole Pine - Zone 3** *(Pinus contorta latifolia)* Slow to moderate growing pine to 50'; long needles, open branching habit.

**Ponderosa Pine - Zone 3** *(Pinus ponderosa 'Southwest')* Difficult to start but hardy once established; not good in wind. Grows 60-80' tall.

**Pinyon Pine - Zone 3** *(Pinus edulis)* Slow growing to 30'; difficult to establish; rounded crown, edible pine nut. Drought tolerant; intermountain native difficult to purchase.

**Scotch Pine - Zone 3** *(Pinus sylvestris)* Grows 70-100' tall; blue-green needles 1½- 3" long; needs water; susceptible to sun burn in winter; irregular growth as they age.

**Vanderwolfe's Pine - Zone 4** *(Pinus flexilis 'Vanderwolfe Pyramid')* Blue green with ascending branches; slow to 20' tall.

**Dwarf Alberta Spruce - Zone 3** *(Picea glauca 'Conica')* Slow to 7' tall; short, soft, bright green needles; needs water and shade; protect from winter sun.

**\*Colorado Spruce - Zone 2** *(Picea pungens glauca)* Best choice for easy to establish very hardy evergreen. Grows 50-115' tall with a beautiful shape and color from green to blue hues.

**\*Fat Albert Spruce - Zone 3** *(Picea pungens 'Fat Albert')* Compact cone shape. Extremely blue and slow growing.

**\*Iseli's Fastigit Spruce - Zone 3** *(Picea pungens fastigiata)* Columnar spruce to 10' with spread of 3'; select blue color.

**\*Hoopsi Spruce - Zone 3** *(Picea pungens glauca 'Hoopsi')* Extremely blue; grows to 20' tall. Nice, thick-shaped, grafted tree; pyramidal form.

*\* Bread & Butter varieties; see page 37*

# DECIDUOUS TREES

**Alder, Mountain - Zone 3** *(Alnus tenuifolia)* Shrub or small tree 20-25' tall.

**Ash, American Mountain - Zone 2** *(Sorbus Americana)* Lacy, dark green leaves, white flower, and red fruit; more disease-resistant than European Mountain Ash. Reddish-Orange fall color.

**Ash, European Mountain - Zone 2** *(Sorbus aucuparia)* 30'x 20'; protect from winter sun, bark will burn; lacy leaf; white flower with orange berries birds enjoy. Red-orange fall color.

**Ash, Mancana - Zone 2** *(Fraxinus mandchurian)* Narrow but dense canopy; dark green foliage; grows to 30' tall.

**\*Aspen, Quaking - Zone 2** *(Populus tremuloides)* Fast to 30' tall. Yellow-orange fall color; intermountain native.

**\*Aspen, Swedish - Zone 2** *(Populus tremula 'Erecta')* Columnar form of European aspen. Brilliant orange-red fall color; tolerates partial shade to sun.

**Birch, Western Red - Zone 3** *(Betula occidentalis fontinalis)* Beautiful, multi-stemmed to 30' tall; red bark.

**\*Canada Red or Schubert Chokecherry Zone 2** *(Prunus virginiana 'Shubertii')* New green growth flushes to purple; fragrant clustered white flower in Spring; nice shape to 25' x 20', wind and drought tolerant. Excellent contrast tree.

**\*Cottonwood, Lanceleaf - Zone 3** *(Populus acuminata)* The best shade tree. Glossy green leaf, pale underneath; fast grower to 45' x 20', very hardy; yellow fall color; extremely wind tolerant. Cottonless.

**\*Cottonwood, Narrowleaf - Zone 3** *(Populus angustifolia)* Fast grower to 30-50' tall; narrow leaf similar to willow, yellow fall color; intermountain native.

**Crabapple** ( see Flowering Crabapple p.40)

**Japanese Tree Lilac - Zone 4** *(Syringa reticulata)* Small tree to 20'x15'; large fragrant white flower; smooth, glossy bark. Must be planted in a protected site.

**Maple, Autumn Blaze - Zone 3** *(Acer freemanii)* Upright oval tree to 50' x 40'; brilliant long-lasting orange-red fall color; prefers some protection from wind.

**\*Maple, Manitoba - Zone 3** *(Acer negundo)* 'Box Elder' - Grows to 60', suckering habit and weak branches, but easily adaptable to many soil conditions; yellow fall color; seeds readily, native.

**Maple, Sensation - Zone 2** *(Acer negundo 'Sensation')* Round headed tree to 30' x 20'; Brilliant red fall color; "Bug proof" "Box Elder".

**Rocky Mountain Maple - Zone 3** *(Acer glabrum)* Multi-trunked to 20-30' tall; shiny green leaves turn pale yellow to orange in fall; more drought-tolerant than other maples; native.

**Mayday Tree - Zone 2** *(Prunus padus)* Green foliage; fragrant clustered white flower; small black fruit; 20' x 15'; prone to winter kill.

**Oak, Bur - Zone 3** *(Quercus macrocarpa)* Broadly oval, irregular shape to 55' x 30'; excellent in alkaline soil; corky branches, large, ornamental acorns, very slow growing.

**\*Willow, Golden - Zone 2** *(Salix alba vitellina)* Fast growing to 60' tall; high water requirement; bright yellow branches.

**\*Willow, Laurel Leaf - Zone 3** *(Salix pentandra)* Fast growing to 30' x 30'; shiny, green foliage; golden yellow fall color; tolerates many soil conditions.

*\* Bread & Butter varieties; see page 37*

# FLOWERING CRABAPPLE VARIETIES

| Name | Size: ( height x width) | Description | Zone |
|---|---|---|---|
| 'Adam's' | rounded, 20x20' | pink bud opens to bright red flower; green leaf with a red tint | 4 |
| 'Baccata' | Common Crabapple | very hardy; white flower, green leaf | 2 |
| 'Klehm's Improved Bechtel' | 25x20' | large, double fragrant, light pink flowers, green leaf; 1¼" sparse green fruit | 4 |
| 'Brandywine' | 20x20' | pink, rose shaped flower; green leaf with mahogany fall color 1¼" green fruit | 4 |
| 'Candied Apple' | Hardy, Weeping variety to 10x15' | abundant pink blossoms, dark green leaf with reddish overcast; persistent cherry-red fruit | 4 |
| 'Centurion' | 20x15' | rose-red flower; dark green leaf with slight overcast to red; small red fruit | 4 |
| 'Dainty' | semi-weeping, grows to 15x20' | abundant pinkish blossoms; purplish-bronze leaves; minimal fruit | 4 |
| 'Dolgo' | 40x40' | very hardy; profuse, single-white flowers; green leaf; flavorful cherry-like clusters of ¼" red fruit | 2 |
| 'Hopa' | 20x25' | upright when young, broadens with age; single rose, pink flower with white star; bronze-green foliage; profuse red fruit good for jelly | 4 |
| 'Indian Magic' | rounded head to 20' | red buds open to deep pink blooms; green leaf; ½" red fruit turns golden orange | 4 |
| 'Indian Summer' | 18x20' | rust resistant variety; rose-red flowers; bronze-green foliage followed by ½" persistent red fruit | 4 |

# FLOWERING CRABAPPLE VARIETIES

| Name | Size ( height x width) | Description | Zone |
|---|---|---|---|
| 'Madonna' | 18x10' | compact, with white gardenia-like blossoms; new growth bronze turning to green leaves; ½" golden /blush red fruit | 4 |
| 'Norraganset' | 15x12' | velvety carmine buds open to white blooms tinged with pink; brilliant red ½" fruit in fall; disease-resistant | 4 |
| 'Prairie Fire' | 20x20' | upright branching pattern; purple to reddish-green leaves; bright pink flower; dark red, ⅜" fruit | 4 |
| 'Profusion' | 10x15' | purplish-red flower with pink center; purple-bronze leaf; profuse maroon fruit | 3 |
| 'Radiant' | 20x15' | very hardy; red bud opens to a deep pink flower; reddish leaf turns to bronze-green; bright red, ½" fruit | 4 |
| 'Red Baron' | 20x15' | columnar variety; bronze bark; good street tree; dark red flower; purple leaf fades to a bronze-gold; broad red berries | 4 |
| 'Red Jade' | Weeping variety 10x15' | deep pink buds open to white flowers; green foliage; glossy, bright red, ½" fruit | 4 |
| 'Robinson' | Upright form to 15' | deep pink flowers; reddish-green leaf; red fruit | 4 |

# FLOWERING CRABAPPLE VARIETIES

| Name | Size ( height x width) | Description | Zone |
|------|------------------------|-------------|------|
| 'Royalty' | 15x15' | very hardy; single, bright-crimson flower; rich-purple foliage; reddish-purple fruit | 2 |
| 'Sargentii' | Dwarf, spreading variety 6-8' x 10-12' | pure white flowers; persistent ¼" dark-red fruit; lobed green foliage | 4 |
| 'Spring Snow' | 25x22' | cleanest variety; snow-white flowers; bright-green leaf; sterile | 4 |
| 'Snow Cloud' | 22x15' | upright vase shaped variety; profuse white bunches of flowers cover entire tree; green leaves; insignificant to non-existent fruit | 4 |
| 'Snowdrift' | 20' | white flower; green leaf; attractive, small ⅜" green and yellow fruit | 3 |
| 'Sugar Tyme' | Upright, spreading to 18' | pale pink buds open to extremely fragrant, single-white flowers; green leaf; persistent ½" red fruit | 4 |
| 'Thunderchild' | 15x15' | single, delicate pink flowers appear before deep purple foliage; dark-red ½" fruit in fall | 3 |

# "BIRDSCAPING"

Birds are attracted to bright colors, fruits, and berries. Areas with dense foliage, water, and shade appeal to them at this elevation. Due to the shortness of our growing season, the few berries that are produced will likely be eaten by our feathered friends before you can get them yourself.

Birds also need winter cover. You can create bird sanctuaries by using a combination of any of these varieties designed to suit your site.

Bird houses and bird feeders are also key to your "Birdscape." Strategically placed, they can provide hours of entertainment!

## PLANTS THAT ATTRACT and PROTECT BIRDS

| Scientific Name | Common Name | Description |
|---|---|---|
| Amelanchier alnifolia | Saskatoon Serviceberry | purple berry in fall |
| Aronia melanocarpa | Black Chokeberry | 1/4" dark berry |
| Artemisia tridentata | Big Sage | winter cover |
| Cotoneaster acutifolia | Peking Cotoneaster | black fruit in fall |
| Cornus sericea | Red 'Osier' Dogwood | green berry |
| Juniper | Rocky Mountain Juniper | pea-sized bluish berries |
| Lonicera | Honeysuckle | bright red summer berries |
| Mahonia repens | Creeping Oregon Grape | blue fruit, late summer |
| Malus | Flowering Crabapple | Assorted fruits and berries |
| | (See Flowering Crabapple List page 40) | |
| Picea pungens | Colorado Spruce | winter cover |
| Prunus padus | Mayday Tree | small black fruit |
| Prunus tomentosa | Nanking Cherry | scarletberry, early summer |
| Prunus virginiana | Chokecherry | dark, edible fruit, late summer |
| Ribes aureum | Golden Current | late summer fruit |
| Ribes 'Red Lake' | Red Lake Current | bright red, edible berry |
| Rosa ssp | Assorted Roses | rose hips throughout, winter cover |
| | (See hardy roses we've tried page 83) | |
| Sambucus | Elderberry | blue-black berry in summer |
| Shepherdia argentia | Buffaloberry | sour orange fruit |
| Sorbus aucuparia | Mountain Ash | orange berry clumps in late summer |
| Symphoricarpos 'alba' | Common Snowberry | white berries in late summer-fall |
| Viburnum dentatum | Arrowood Viburnum | blue-black berries |
| Viburnum trilobum | American Cranberry | scarlet berries, summer |
| Viburnum trilobum | Wentwerth | heavy fruiting variety |

Sunflowers, Sagebrush, Rabbitbrush, Gooseberry

## SHRUBS:  DECIDUOUS AND EVERGREEN

Shrubs/bushes are your fillers. They are the unsung heroes in the landscape. Great for privacy screens, wind barriers, accents, texture, color, and transitions from manicured to wild (natural) areas, from trees to flower beds, as well as "birdscaping" elements.

As a group, shrubs perform better than trees at elevation due to the nature of their form - clumping and suckering.

Decide you like shrubs when you move to a mountainous region. There are varieties from 25' tall all the way to creeping - literally, a shrub for every reason.

There are people who prefer planting only native plants. We recommend some natives, but as a whole, they are very slow growing, very difficult to establish and somewhat stubborn to keep alive in containers until they are sold due to their coarse root structure. When they are transplanted or relocated, they have an extremely low survivability - dropping below 50%. In short, a bit overrated. Consequently, we have chosen many native-like plants that are cold-hardy but more user-friendly and varied (with similarities but better transplant survival rates) -to add dimension to your landscape.

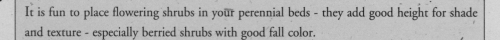

It is fun to place flowering shrubs in your perennial beds - they add good height for shade and texture - especially berried shrubs with good fall color.

Our Mountain-Desert Shrub Picks by height are:

## —— LOW GROWING SHRUBS TO 30" TALL ——

| ZONE | VARIETY/ SPECIES | DESCRIPTION |
|------|------------------|-------------|
| 4 | "Crimson Pygmy" Barberry- *Berberis thunbergii atropurpurea nana* | protect from wind; excellent foundation plant, blood red leaves, 24" tall |
| 4 | Rose Glow Barberry- *Berberis thunbergii* | new growth light variegated, pink dark rose red at maturity 30"- 40" tall; protect from wind. |
| 3 | Dogwood, Dwarf Kelseyi - *Cornus sericea 'Kelseyi'* | Dwarf red twig variety to 24"; nice shade groundcover |
| | Juniper - *Juniperus horizontalis* | |
| 3 | 'Bar Harbor'- 12" x 6' | steel blue; wine color in winter; salt tolerant |
| 3 | 'Blue Chip' - 8"x 6' | slate blue; plum in winter; dense ground cover |
| 2 | 'Prince of Wales' - 6"x10' | soft blue green; low spreader |
| 3 | 'Wiltonii' (Blue Rug) - 4" x 6' | frosty blue; good slope stabilizer; very flat; dense |
| 3 | 'Youngstown' - 18" x 6' | blue-green/ plume-like |
| | Juniper - *Juniperus communis depressa* | |
| 2 | 'Effusa' - 12" x 6' | tolerates shade |
| | Juniper - *Juniperus sabina* | |
| 3 | 'Arcadia' - 12" x 8' | bright green; lacy texture |
| 3 | 'Broadmoor' - 12" x 6' | soft gray-green; low mound |
| 3 | 'Buffalo'- 12" x 8' | bright green; feathery |
| 3 | 'Scandia' - 12" x 6' | pale gray-green; good winter color |
| 3 | 'Sierra Spreader' - 12" x 5' | bright green; lacy, good winter color |
| 4 | 'Tam' - 30" x 6' | blue-green, matures to green; fast-growing |
| 4 | 'New Blue Tam' - 21" x 6' | outstanding blue foliage |

# LOW GROWING SHRUBS TO 30" TALL

| ZONE | VARIETY/ SPECIES | DESCRIPTION |
|------|------------------|-------------|
| 4 | Oregon Grape, Creeping - *Mahonia repens* | yellow flower, blue berry, red fall color, holly-like leaf, drought-tolerant |
| 5 | Sage, Russian - *Perovskia atriplicifolia* | lavender flower, silvery foliage, cut after frost; tender at this elevation |
| | Spirea - *Spiraea* | |
| 4 | 'Anthony Waterer' - *Spiraea bumalda* | dark pink flower late spring, green-bronze foliage |
| 4 | 'Crispa' - *Spiraea bumalda* | leaves are deeply serrated for lacy appearance |
| 4 | 'Goldflame' - *Spiraea bumalda* | bronze growth matures to yellow; pink flower |
| 4 | 'Grefsheim' - *Spiraea cineria* | 2-3' w/ cascading white flowers in spring |
| 4 | 'Little Princess' - *Spiraea japonica* | clustered light-pink flower, green foliage |
| 4 | 'Snowmound' - *Spiraea nipponica* | bluish-green leaves; round white cluster flowers |
| 3 | Snowberry - *Symphoricarpos alba* | pinkish flower, white berry in fall; to 3' |
| 2 | Potentilla - *Potentilla cinquefoil* | fast-growing; flowers from cream to red, 2-5' tall |
| 2 | 'Abbottswood'- *Potentilla fruticosa* | large white flower, densely spreading, 2-3' tall, 2-3' wide |
| 2 | 'Coronation Triumph'- *Potentilla fruticosa* | bright-yellow, 3-4' tall, 2-3' wide, mounded one, of the earliest bloomers |
| 2 | 'Gold Drop'- *Potentilla fruticosa* | abundant lemon-yellow, 2' tall, 2-3' wide, compact, fernlike foliage |
| 2 | 'Jackmanii'- *Potentilla fruticosa* | deep-yellow blooms, 3-4' tall, 3-4' wide, rounded, coarse dark-green foliage |

# LOW GROWING SHRUBS TO 30" TALL

| ZONE | VARIETY/ SPECIES | DESCRIPTION |
|---|---|---|
| 2 | 'Katherine Dykes'-*Potentilla fruticosa* | soft yellow blooms, 2-3' tall, 3-4' wide, spreading, arching, gray-green foliage |
| 3 | 'Mckay's White'-*Potentilla fruticosa* | creamy-white flowers, 2-2½' tall, 2-3' wide, mounded, soft-green foliage |
| 2 | 'Snowbird'-*Potentilla fruticosa* | 80% double white; 20% single-white 2-2 ½' tall 2-3' wide; upright, compact; clean, glossy foliage |
| 2 | 'Yellow Gem'-*Potentilla fruticosa* | bright-yellow 1-2'tall x 3-4'wide; low spreading; gray, hairy foliage |
| 2 | 'Pink Beauty'-*Potentilla fruticosa* | pale-pink blooms, 2-3'tall x 2-3'wide; mounded; green foliage; stays pinker in part shade |

*Big Sage*

# MEDIUM GROWING SHRUBS 3' TO 6' TALL

| ZONE | VARIETY/ SPECIES | DESCRIPTION |
|---|---|---|
| 3 | Cistena Plum - *Prunus cistena* | purple leaf, multi-branched to 5'; pink flower in spring |
| 2 | Alpine Currant - *Ribes alpinum* | 3-5' hedge; dense growth; shiny green leaves |
| 3 | Golden Currant - *Ribes aureum* | 3-5'; edible berries; yellow-orange fall color |
| 3 | Indian Currant - *Symphoricarpos orbiculatus* | 4-5' branches arch with weight of red fruit |
| 2 | Buffaloberry-*Shepherdia argentia* | 6'; gray foliage; drought tolerant; sour, edible fruit |
| 3 | Dwarf Burning Bush - *Euonymus compacta alata* | 4-6' needs protected site; bright-red fall color |
| 3 | Red 'Osier Dogwood' - *Cornus sericea* | bright red branches; white flowers; prune to keep hedge low, needs moisture |
| 3 | Variegated Dogwood - *Cornus alba* | compact, variegated Red Twig to 4-5' |
| 4 | Flowering Almond - *Prunus glandulosa* | 2-5'; fragrant double-pink spring flower |
| 2 | Hi-graft Globosa - *Picea pungens glauca* | evergreen mound to 3'; blue spruce on a stick |
| 3 | Clavey's Honeysuckle - *Lonicera xylosteum* | slow growing to 4'; fragrant white flower in spring; red berries |
| 3 | Mini globe Honeysuckle -*L. xylosteoides* | to 3', dense green foliage; compact |
| 4 | Mountain Mahogany -*Cercocarpus montanus* | 3-10'; drought-tolerant; dark-green leaves; difficult to establish, native |
| 3 | Curlleaf Mahogany - *Cercocarpus ledifolius* | 6'; leathery, narrow leaves; drought-tolerant; difficult to establish; native |
| 2 | Common Ninebark - *Physocarpus opulifolius* | white flowers; red pods; yellow fall color; can die back to ground annually |

# MEDIUM GROWING SHRUBS 3' TO 6' TALL

| ZONE | VARIETY/ SPECIES | DESCRIPTION |
|---|---|---|
| 2 | Dwarf Mugo Pine - *Pinus 'mugo pumilio'* | dark green dense mound; slow to 4' |
| 3 | Japanese Red Pine - *'Jane Klus'* | similar to Mugo Pine with yellow hue |
| 2 | Potentilla - *Potentilla cinquefoil* (see Low Growing Shrubs List page 46) | profuse yellow, white, pink, orange flowers |
| 2-4 | Roses - (see Rose List page 83) | assorted colors and bloom times |
| 3 | Rubber Rabbitbrush - *Chrysothamnus nauseosus* | brilliant gold fall flowers; drought tolerant, 2 - 4'; native |
| 3 | Big Sage - *Artemisia tridentata* | evergreen shrub to 4'; drought tolerant; strongly aromatic; native |
| 2 | Western Sandcherry - *Prunus besseyi* | fragrant white flower; black berry; wind, heat, and cold tolerant |
| 3 | Dwarf Scotch Pine - *Pinus sylvestris glauca 'nana' waterii* | rounded blue-green evergreen |
| 3 | Common Snowball- *Viburnum opulus roseum* | protect from wind; large balls white-green of flowers |
| 2 | Ashleaf Spirea - *Sorbaria sorbifolia* | fern-like foliage; plumes of off white flowers, may die back some in winter |
| 4 | Vanhoutte Spirea - *Spiraea vanhouttei* | fountain shaped shrub; blue-green foliage |
| 5 | Nest Spruce - *Picea abies nidiformis* | flattened globe evergreen; 3' x 4' |
| 3 | Sumac - *Rhus trilobata* | wind, heat, drought-tolerant; red fall color |
| 2 | Viburnum - *Viburnum dentatum* 'Arrow Wood' | 5-8'; excellent for wet soils; red fall color |
| 2 | Viburnum - *Viburnum trilobum* 'Bailey Compact' | 5-6'; deep red fall color |
| 4 | Arctic Blue Willow - *Salix purpurea nana* | 4-8'; whispy blue-green foliage, wind-tolerant; requires water |
| 4 | Scotch Broom - *Cytisus coparicus* | 3- 6'; golden-yellow flowers, upright stems |

# TALL GROWING SHRUBS TO 6' PLUS

| ZONE | VARIETY/ SPECIES | DESCRIPTION |
|---|---|---|
| 2 | Chokecherry - *Prunus virginiana* | wind, drought tolerant; showy white flower; edible fruit; 15-20'; suckering habit |
| 2 | Schubert Chokecherry- *Prunus v. schuberti* | new growth green turning to purple; clusters of white flowers, minimal fruit |
| 3 | Black Chokeberry - *Aronia melanocarpa* | tolerates cold, heat, wet soil, wind; suckering to 10'; fruit in fall |
| 2 | Nanking Cherry - *Prunus tomentosa* | pink spring flower; edible fruit; 8' x 10', soft, green foliage |
| 3 | Peking Cotoneaster - *Cotoneaster acutifolia* | small, shiny leaves; red/orange fall color; black berry; attractive shape |
| 2 | Native American Cranberry - *Viburnum trilobum* | red berry and red fall color, lacy flower |
| 2 | Red 'Osier' Dogwood - *Cornus sericea* | bright red branches; white spring flower; purplish/red fall color |
| 3 | Elderberry - *Sambucus* | bright green foliage; blue/black fruit excellent for pies |
| 3 | Golden Elderberry -*Sambuous canadensis* | golden foliage, edible red fruit follows white blooms; 8' x 8' |
| 3 | Honeysuckle - *Lonicera* | tolerates all soil conditions; very hardy |
| 3 | 'Arnold Red' - *L. tatarica* | dark-red flowers bright-red fruit |
| 3 | 'Honeyrose' - *L. zylosteum* | rosy-red flower; 10'tall 8-10' wide |
| 3 | 'Freedom' - *L. Freedom* | white flower; bluish foliage |
| 3 | 'Zabel's' - *L. tatarica* | dark-red cultivar; red fall fruit |

# —— TALL GROWING SHRUBS TO 6' PLUS ——

| ZONE | VARIETY/ SPECIES | DESCRIPTION |
|---|---|---|
| 4 | Juniper - *chinensis* - Spearmint 15' x 5' | columnar; rich green |
| 4 | -*media*- Hetzii 15' tall | |
| | -*Juniperus scopulorum* - | blue-gray; arching |
| 3 | 'Rocky Mountain' 15' x 6' | blue-green; tolerates wind and drought |
| 3 | 'Gray Gleam' 15' x 6' | soft, silvery; symmetrical |
| 3 | 'Moonglow' 15' x 6' | silver-gray; broad; pyramidal |
| 3 | 'Table Top Blue' 6' x 8' | silver-gray; excellent hedge |
| 4 | 'Skyrocket' to 20' | silver-gray; very narrow to |
| 3 | 'Welchii' 8' x narrow | silvery-green, |
| 3 | 'Wichita Blue' 20' tall | dense blue; very narrow |
| | | bright steel-blue, wide pyramid |
| | Lilac - (See Lilac List page 52) | assorted colors |
| 3 | Upright, Standard Mugo Pine- | dwarf upright pine to 10' |
| | Swiss Mountain Pine -*Pinus rostrada* | |
| 4 | Scrub Oak - *Quercus gambelii* | difficult to establish; drought tolerant; native, grows faster with irrigation |
| 2 | Siberian Peashrub - *Caragana arborescens* | tolerates wind, heat, poor soil; yellow sweet pea flower followed by pea pod; delicate shaped leaves |
| 2 | Serviceberry - *Amelanchier alnifolia* | white flower, edible deep purple fruit; new growth red/bronze |
| 3 | Smooth Sumac - *Rhus glabra* | smooth bark; fern-like leaves; orange/red color; to 8' |
| 3 | Staghorn Sumac - *Rhus typhina* | deep-green leaf; red fall color; to 15'; dies back in winter |

# —— HARDY LILACS ——

| ZONE | VARIETY/ SPECIES | DESCRIPTION |
|---|---|---|
| 3 | Chinese Lilac - *Syringa chinensis saugeana* | vigorous, dense, upright lilac to 10' x 6-8'; Rich, airy open clusters of blossoms; non-suckering |
| 2 | Common Lilac - *Syringa vulgaris* | 15- 20' x 15-20' pinkish bloom |
| 2 | French Lilac - *Syringa vulgaris ssp*<br>'Charles Joly' - double,dark purple/red<br>'Ellen Willmott' - double, white<br>'Katherine Havemeyer' - double pink<br>'Ludwig Spaeth' - single, purple<br>'Madame Lemoine' - double, white<br>'My Favorite' - dark purple<br>'President Lincoln' - single, blue<br>'Sensation' - purple with white edge<br>'President Grevy' - double blue | flowers a little later than common lilac large clusters of single or double showy flowers |
| 2 | Hardy Lilac - *Syringa prestoniae*<br>'James McFarlane'-pink<br>'Donald Wyman'-lavender<br>'Miss Canada'-bright pink<br>'Minuet'-purple bud opens to light pink | grows to 8-12' x same width. Extra hardy developed in Canada; blooms 2 weeks later than *vulgaris* and can tolerate more moisture; Semi-textured green leaf. |

# HARDY LILACS

| ZONE | VARIETY/ SPECIES | DESCRIPTION |
|---|---|---|
| 2 | Hybrid Lilac - *Syringa hyacinthiflora* 'Mt. Baker'-white 'Pocahontas'-purple | hybrid vulgaris and chinese lilac to 10-12'; noted for extreme hardiness; blooms earlier than French Hybrids; could be a down fall at higher elevation. |
| 4 | Japanese Tree Lilac - *Syringa reticulata* | small tree to 20x15';. extremely large, white flowers in early summer; needs protection from the wind. |
| 3 | Dwf. Korean Lilac - *Syringa meyeri 'Palibin'* | Dwarf Lilac to 5x5-7'; Fragrant lilac lavender flowers profuse at an early age, to 12x12' wide. |
| 3 | Late Lilac - *Syringa villosa* | Hardy, late blooming lilac. Rosy, lilac blooms in late spring contrast with a textured green leaf. |
| 4 | Miss Kim Lilac - *Syringa vilutina 'Miss Kim'* | Dwarf Lilac to 3'; Small lavender blossom in early summer. Tolerates shade |

*"The real voyage of discovery consists not in seeking new landscapes, but in having new eyes."*

-unknown

# PERENNIAL DESIGN CONCEPTS

Color transforms an ordinary yard into a garden. It brings life and interest to planting areas and helps focus and draw your vision around the yard.

These are your seasonal eye-catchers. Try to wait until your trees and shrubs are in place before planting flowers. It can be difficult to plant large trees and shrubs amongst your flowers plus trees and shrubs will change your sun and wind exposures - usually for the better. Choose some appropriate ornamentals with varying heights and textures (i.e. Flowering Crabapple, Canada Redcherry, Aspen-Singles and Clumps, unique Evergreens, Amur Maple, Shade Trees, etc.)

After properly preparing your planting area (as described earlier in How to: page 3) and placing your height and texture plants, you are ready to plan and design your perennial garden.

## Keep in mind:

- Sun Requirement
- Color
- Bloom time- Early Spring/Spring/Late Spring-Summer/Summer/
  Late Summer-Fall
- Foliage texture
- Plant heights - low growing, medium, tall

Gardening is truly a matter of opinion. Some people prefer strictly "cool" colors - blues, purples, pastels, white. Other people like "hot" colors - red, yellow, orange, bright pink. . .

Pick colors you want to look at in each spot. Sometimes you will want to compromise your color scheme in order to have something blooming in a specific site during a specific season. Please don't hate a color, simply choose not to use it in your yard. Accept other people's opinions so they can acknowledge yours.

Nature has created indescribable and inimitable shades of all colors. There are many guidelines for 'matching' these colors but, ultimately, it is the choice of the gardener. Go for some combinations! Be flexible with your plan - it's more fun that way. When you go to buy and there is something interesting to try, make a spot for it.

As a general guideline, plant in groups of 1, 3, 5, 7, etc. of each variety. If a plant has an invasive quality or gets very large be sure to give it enough space, and use fewer of them. Space from 6" to 24" apart. READ THE TAGS - there is a lot of valuable information on them.

## DESIGN IDEAS

In designing an area, you can make statements with varying heights and bloom groupings. Your eye will go to wherever the color is that season. Try not to hide low growing varieties behind taller ones - unless you are going for the "peek-a-boo" tactic.

### Diagram A: Grouping Garden

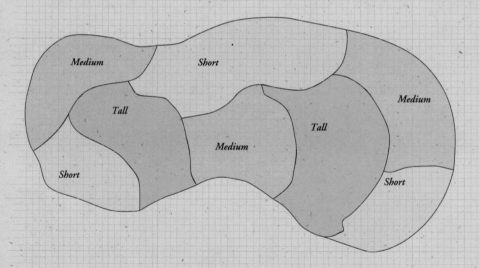

Another plan may be putting taller varieties toward the center and tapering down (The Bulls-Eye Plan) toward the border - Full View Garden.

*Diagram B:  Full Veiw Garden*

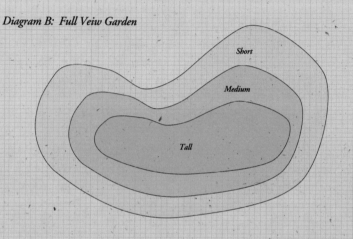

Or, you may want to put taller varieties with varying bloom times in back with medium sized, varying blooms next, and bordering the bed with low-growing varieties with varying bloom times.

*Diagram C:  Front Veiw Garden*

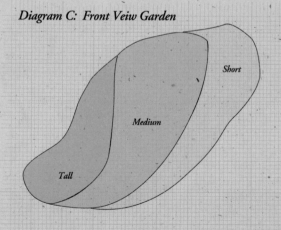

# PERENNIAL PLANT CHOICES

If you choose plants from each bloom period with varying heights and textures, you should have a respectable representation of seasonal color in your yard.

## —————— PERENNIALS BY BLOOM TIME ——————
*\* biennial or half hardy perennial*
*\*\* ground covers*

Legend (left margin):
- ◐ Root Shade
- ◑ Partial Sun
- ● Full Shade
- ⊛ Full Sun

| Sun Requirement | Variety | Height | Description |
|---|---|---|---|
| | **Early Spring** | | |
| ⊛ ◐ | Crocus | 6" | great array of sizes and colors |
| ⊛ ◐ | Daffodil-*Narcissus* | 6-18" | yellow, pink, white, orange |
| ⊛ ◐ | Grape Hyacinth-*Muscari* | 6" | white, purple, pink |
| ⊛ ◐ | Pansies,Viola-*Viola* | *2-10" | mixed colors |
| ◐ | Primrose-*Primula* | 6" | most colors |
| ⊛ ◐ | Lenten Rose-*Helleborus* | 6-18" | white, purple, pink |
| ◐ | Snowdrop-*Galanthus* | 6-10" | white |
| ⊛ ◐ | Tulip-*Tulipa* | 6"-2' | all colors |
| | **Spring** | | |
| ⊛ ◐ | Aster-Alpine | 12" | purple |
| | Goliath | 15" | blue |
| | Wartburg Star | 12" | pink |
| ⊛ ◐ | Basket of Gold-*Alyssum* | | |
| | *saxatile* | 12" | golden yellow |
| ◐ ◑ | Bergenia-*Bergenia* | 12-18" | pink, large leathery leaf |
| ⊛ | Candytuft-*Iberis* | 9-12" | white, pinkish |
| ⊛ ◐ | Peachleaf bellflower- | | |
| | *Campanula persicifolia* | 20" | purple, white, blue |
| ⊛ ◐ | Columbine-*Aquilegia* | 6"-3' | mixed colors |
| ⊛ | Cushion Spurge-*Euphorbia* | 18" | greenish yellow bracts |
| ● ◐ | Forget-me-nots - *Myosotis* | 6-18" | blue and very small |
| ⊛ ◐ | Leopard's Bane- *Doronicum* | 12" | yellow |
| ● | Lily-of-the-Valley-*Convallaria* | 8" | white |
| ● ◐ | Pasque Flower-*Anemone* | 8-12" | blue-reddish purple |
| ⊛ | Peony-*Paeonia* | 18"-3' | pink, white, red, lavender |
| ⊛ ◐ | Phlox, Creeping-*Phlox* | 6" | pink, white, blue, lavender |

# PERENNIALS BY BLOOM TIME
### * biennial or half hardyperennial
### ** ground covers

| Sun Requirement | Variety | Height | Description |
|---|---|---|---|
| | | | |

## Late Spring-Summer

| Sun Requirement | Variety | Height | Description |
|---|---|---|---|
| ◐ | Ajuga-*Ajuga reptans* | **6" | bronze-green foliage/ spike blue flower |
| ○ ◐ | Rock Cress-*Arabis* | **6" | pink, white, rose, lavender |
| ● ◐ | Yellow Archangel *Lamiastrum galeobdolon* | **8-12" | yellow flower, variegated foliage |
| ○ ◐ | Artemisia-*Artemisia* | | |
| | Silvermound | 15-24" | mounding silver-gray plant |
| | Silver Brocade | **3" | creeping to 12", silver-gray foliage |
| ● ◐ | Bluebells-*Mertensia* | 12-24" | blue |
| ○ | Blue Flax-*Linum lewisi* | 18"-3' | blue |
| ● ○ | *Brunnera* | 12-18" | pale blue Forget-me-not, heart shaped |
| ● ◐ | Buttercup, Creeping- *Ranunculus* | **6-12" | yellow |
| ○ | Catmint-*Nepeta* | 12-24" | purple to lavender spikes |
| ○ ◐ | Coral Bells-*Heuchera* | 12-24" | red, white, and coral |
| | Daisy- *Chrysanthemum* | 6" | |
| | English Bell | **4" | mixed colors |
| | Mat | 1-2' | white/striped |
| | Ox-eye | 12-24" | white |
| | Pyrethrum(Painted) | 24-36" | mixed colors |
| ○ ◐ | Dame's Rocket-*Hesperis* | | mauve to purple and white |
| ○ | Dianthus- *Dianthus* | 18" | |
| | Barbatus | 6-8" | mixed colors |
| | Deltoides | 18" | white, rose, red, salmon |
| | Knappii | 6-8" | yellow |
| | Spotti | 4-6" | red-white spots |
| | Tiny Rubies | 6-8" | pink |
| ○ | Edelweiss-*Leontopodium* | 2-4' | grey foliage; white bracht |
| ○ ◐ | False Lupine-*Thermopsis* | | yellow |

# PERENNIALS BY BLOOM TIME
* biennial or half hardyperennial
** ground covers

| Sun Requirement | Variety | Height | Description |
|---|---|---|---|
| | | | |

## Late Spring-Summer

| Sun Requirement | Variety | Height | Description |
|---|---|---|---|
| ◌ | Fleabane-*Erigeron* | 10-18" | blue, yellow center |
| ● | Foam Flower-*Tiarella* | 6-12" | pink buds to white flowers |
| ◌ ◐ | Foxglove-*Digitalis* | *18"-3' | yellow, white, pink, apricot, purple |
| ◐ ● | Goatsbeard-*Aruncus* | 12"-5' | Astilbe-like plumes on feathery foliage |
| ◌ ◐ | Geranium-*Cranesbill* | 12-20" | hardy varieties: Pink, white, bright blue |
| | *Endressii* | 15-18" | wargrave pink, salmon pink flowers |
| | *Himalayense* | 10-15" | violet blue |
| | *Sanguineum* | 9-12" | magenta, red fall foliage |
| ◐ | Globeflower-*Trollius* | 24-36" | large orange buttercup |
| ◐ | Green Carpet-*Hernaria* | **3" | tiny leaves, can be walked on |
| ◌ ◐ | Iris-*Iris* (German and Siberian) | 6"-3' | most colors |
| ◐ | Honeysuckle, Scarlet Dropmore | Vine | red-orange, rose |
| ● ◐ | Jacobs Ladder-*Polemonium* | 12-24" | blue, white |
| ◌ ◐ | Jupiter's Beard-*Centranthus* | 24" | rose, white |
| ◌ ◐ | Lupine-*Lupinus* | 18"-3' | yellow, red, purple, white, pink |
| ◌ ◐ | Mock Strawberry-*Duchesnia* | **2-3" | small strawberry foliage, yellow flowers, bitter fruit |
| ● ◐ | Moss-*Sagina subulata* | **flat | Irish-dark green; Scotch-light green |
| ● ◐ | Pachysandra | **9-12" | dark glossy leaves, white spike flowers |
| ◌ | Penstemon-*Penstemon* | 8"-4' | orange, rose, pink, purple, blue |
| ◌ ◐ | Potentilla-*Verna* | **flat | green foliage, small yellow flowers |
| | Miss Willmott | **10-12" | red flower, strawberry-like foliage |
| ● ◐ | Prunella, Loveliness | 4-10" | lavender, pink, rounded foliage |
| | Self-heal | 4-10" | lavender, serrated foliage |

60

* biennial or half hardyperennial
** ground covers

| Sun Requirement | Variety | Height | Description |
|---|---|---|---|
| | | | |

## Late Spring-Summer

| Sun Requirement | Variety | Height | Description |
|---|---|---|---|
| ◌ | Poppy, Alpine | *8-10" | yellow, red, white, peach, pink |
| | Iceland | *12-18" | yellow, white, pink, apricot, orange |
| | Oriental | 18-24" | orange, scarlet, pink, salmon, white |
| ◌ ◑ | Pussy Toes-*Antennaria* | 8-10" | silver mound with pink paw-like flowers |
| ◌ | Rock Cress-*Arabis* | **6" | white, rose, pink |
| | *Aubrieta* | **6-8" | pink, blue, red, purple, violet |
| ◑ | Sandwort-*Arenaria* | **6" | white, mossy carpet |
| ◌ ◑ | Sea Thirft-*Armeria* | **6-8" | pink pom-pom flowers grass foliage |
| ◌ ◑ | Sedum- Blue Spruce | **3" | yellow, blue spruce-like foliage |
| | Blue Ridge | **1" | bluish color, creeper |
| | Dragon's Blood | **4" | green-red foliage, rose flower |
| | Gray Button | **3" | gray foliage, white flower |
| | Kamtschaticum | **3" | yellow flower, green foliage, variegated foliage also |
| | Red Carpet | **4" | red foliage, red flower |
| | Tri-color | **3" | variegated red, green, white striking foliage |
| | Utah | **3" | yellow star-like flowers; green foliage |
| ◑ ● | Spiderwort-*Tradescantia* | 1-3" | purple, white |
| ◑ ● | Soapwort-*Saponaria* | **3" | profuse pink flowers |
| ◑ ● | Snow-in-Summer-*Cerastium* | ** 6-8" | white, silver foliage |
| ◌ | Sulphur Flower-*Eriogonum* | 5" | densly clumped yellow tufts |
| ◑ ● | Sweet Woodruff-*Galium* | **6-8" | tiny white flowers, bright green foliage |
| ◑ ● | Wild Strawberry-*Fragaria* | **3-6" | ground cover, deep pink |

# PERENNIALS BY BLOOMTIME

\* biennial or half hardyperennial

\*\* ground covers

| Sun Requirement | Variety | Height | Description |
|---|---|---|---|
| | | | |

## Summer

| Sun Requirement | Variety | Height | Description |
|---|---|---|---|
| ◌ | Anchusa-*Anchusa azurea* | 18-36" | vivid blue, short-lived |
| ◑ ● | Astilbe-*Astilbe* | 12-18" | red, white, lilac, pink |
| ◌ | Baby's Breath-*Gypsophila* | 4-36" | white, pink |
| ◌ | Balloon flower-*Platycodon* | 12-36" | blue, white |
| ◑ ● | Beacon Silver-*Lamium* | \*\*4" | variegated leaves, white-pink flowers |
| ◑ ● | Bishop's Weed-*Aegopodium* | \*\*8-24" | light green leaves/white edges, white lacy flower |
| ◑ ● | Bleeding Heart-*Dicentra* | 18"-3' | pink, white |
| | Fernleaf | 9-18" | pink |
| ◌ | Campanula, Blue Clips | 5" | blue, white, rounded leaf |
| | *Glomerata Superba* | 20" | purple, feathery leaf |
| ◌ | Centaurea-*Dealbata* | 18-24" | fringed pink flowers |
| | Montana blue | 18-24" | violet-blue |
| ◌ | Chives - *Allium schoenoprasum* | 24" | pink clusters on grassy leaves |
| ◑ ● | Creeping Jenny-*Lysimachia* | \*\*2" | yellow buttercup flowers, yellow-green leaves |
| ◐ ◌ | Clematis-*Clematis* | Vine | purple, white, pink, red |
| ◌ | Daisy -*Chrysanthemum* | | |
| | Shasta | 12"-4' | white varieties-assorted |
| ◑ ◌ | Cupid's Dart-*Catanache* | 18-30" | white, blue |
| ◑ ◌ | Delphinium-*Delphinium* | 12"-4' | white, pinks, blues |
| ◑ ◌ | False Indigo - *Baptista* | 3-5' | blue flowers |
| ◑ ◌ | Geum-*Geum* | 12-24" | yellow, orange-red |
| ◌ | Goldilocks-*Rudbeckia* | 10" | double gold |
| ◌ | Hens-n-Chicks-*Sempervivum* | \*\* 3" | tightly packed rosettes, succulent |
| ◑ ◌ | Hosta-*Hosta* | 3-24" | white, pink and lavender, leafy foliage |

# PERENNIALS BY BLOOM TIME

\* biennial or half hardyperennial
\*\* ground covers

| Sun Requirement | Variety | Height | Description |
|---|---|---|---|
| | | | |

## Summer

| Sun Req. | Variety | Height | Description |
|---|---|---|---|
| ◑ ● | Lady's Mantle-*Alchemilla* | 4-6" | lobed, grey-green leaves |
| ◍ | Liatris-*Liatris* 'Gay-feather' | 28" | rosy-pink bottle brush blooms |
| ◍ | Maltese Cross-*Lychnis* | 2-3' | red-orange |
| ◍ ◑ | Meadow Rue-*Thalictrum* | 24-36" | pink, blue |
| ◍ ◑ | Meadow Sweet-*Fillipendula* | 24" | pink, white, red plume |
| ◍ | Mexican Hat-*Ratibida* | 48" | yellow-orange |
| ◍ | Pincushion-*Scabiosa* | 18" | pink, blue, white |
| ◑ ◑ ● | Primrose, Evening-*Oenothera* | 12-30" | yellow |
| ◑ ◑ ● | Purple Palace-*Heuchera* | 8-12" | bronze-purple foliage; white flower |
| ◍ | Rose Campion-*Lychnis* | *2-3' | hot pink, white |
| ◍ | Salvia-*Salvia* | 16-24" | purple, white, pink |
| ◍ ◑ | Speedwell-*Veroncia* | 12-18" | blue, purple, white, pink |
| ◑ ◑ ● | Spiderwort-*Tradescantia* | 18-24" | blue, white, magenta |
| ◍ | Summer Sun-*Heliopsis* | 3' | golden yellow |
| ◍ | Sun Rose-*Helianthemum* | **6-12" | red, apricot, yellow, pink |
| ◍ ◑ | Thyme-Lemon | **4" | green, white leaves |
| | Silver | **3" | variegated leaves |
| | Woolly | **2-3" | low mat, bright lavender |
| | Mother of | **2-6" | purple, aromatic |
| | Creeping | **flat | creeping mat |
| | Lime | **4-10" | lavender |
| ◍ ◑ | Veronia-*Veronica* | 12-18" | blue, rose |
| | Repens | **2" | low mat, white flowers |
| ◑ ● | Vinca Minor-*Vinca* | **2" | glossy green leaves, purple flower |
| ◍ | Wallflower-*Erysimum* | *6-10" | mauve, orange |
| ◍ | Yarrow-*Achillea* | 18-24" | yellow, red, pastels, white |

# PERENNIALS BY BLOOM TIME

\* biennial or half hardyperennial

\*\* ground covers

| Sun Requirement | Variety | Height | Description |
|---|---|---|---|
| | | | |

## Late Summer-Fall

| Sun Requirement | Variety | Height | Description |
|---|---|---|---|
| ⚬ | Aster-Alert | 8-10" | red |
| | Peter Harrison | 16" | pink |
| | Prof. Kippenberg | 14" | lavender blue |
| ◗ ● | Bee Balm-*Monarda* | 24-48" | red, violet, pink |
| ⚬ | Blanket Flower-*Gaillardia* | 6-10" | yellow, burgundy, gold, maroon |
| ⚬ ◗ | Boltonia | 3-4' | white, aster-like |
| ⚬ ◗ | Carnation-*Dianthus* | 6-14" | red, pink, yellow, white |
| ⚬ | Coneflower-*Echinacea* | 18-36" | purple, white |
| ⚬ | Coreopsis-*Coreopsis* | 6-24" | yellow |
| | Tickseed, Lanceleaf, Rosea | | pale yellow, golden, pink |
| ⚬ | Golden Marguerite-*Anthemis* | 30" | yellow, daisy-like |
| ⚬ ◗ | Daylily-*Hemerocallis* | 18-30" | pink, yellow, orange, red, rust; many repeat bloomers |
| ⚬ | Goldenrod-*Solidago* | 18" | golden yellow |
| ⚬ | Goldstrum-*Rudbeckia* | 12-30" | yellow, Black-Eyed Susan |
| ⚬ | Hollyhock-*Alcea* | \*3-6' | assorted |
| ⚬ | Mallow-*Malva* | 24-36" | rose, white |
| ◗ ● | Monkshood-*Aconitum* | 24-36" | purple |
| ⚬ ◗ | Garden Mum-*Chrysanthemum* | \*6-14" | most colors |
| ⚬ ◗ | Obedient Plant-*Physostegia* | 24-48" | pink, white |
| ⚬ | Garden Phlox-*Phlox paniculata* | 18-32" | white, pink, blue, red, mauve |
| ⚬ | Red Hot Poker-*Tritoma* | 36" | tri-color: red, orange, yellow |
| ⚬ | Russian Sage-*Perovskia* | \*24-48" | lavender spikes |
| ⚬ | Sneezeweed-*Helenium* | 18-24" | yellow, orange, red |
| ⚬ ◗ | Statice, German-*Limonium* | 18-20" | white |
| ⚬ | Sedum-Autumn joy | 18-24" | pink |
| | Moorchen | 15" | waxy, bronze foliage |
| | Vera Jameson | 10-12" | waxy, bluish foliage; pink flowers |

# PERENNIALS BY BLOOM TIME

* biennial or half hardyperennial
** ground covers

| Sun Requirement | Variety | Height | Description |
|---|---|---|---|
| | | | |

## Late Summer-Fall

| Sun Requirement | Variety | Height | Description |
|---|---|---|---|
| ◌ ◑ | Perennial Sweet Pea-*Lathyrus* | Vine | rose pink, white |
| ◌ | Tansy-*Tanacetum* | 36" | yellow; noxious weed in some states |
| ◌ ◑ | Virginia Creeper-*Parthenocissus* | Vine | red fall color |

## Grasses:

| Sun Requirement | Variety | Height | Description |
|---|---|---|---|
| ◌ ◑ | Blue Oat Grass- *Avena* | 20-36" | arching blue-gray foliage |
| ◌ | Blue Fescue-*Festuca Ovina* | 10" | compact, bright blue |
| ◌ | Ribbon Grass-*Phalaris* | 24-36" | arching bright green-white foliage |
| ◌ | Blue Lyme Grass-*Elymus glaucus* | 24-26" | blue-gray foliage |

## Fern:

| Sun Requirement | Variety | Height | Description |
|---|---|---|---|
| ● | Male Fern-*Dryopteris* | 24" | drought tolerant once established check for restrictions, zone 4 |
| ◑ ● | Royal Fern-*Osmunda* | 24" | hardy, zone 2, slow spreading |
| ◑ ● | Lady Fern-*Athyrium* | 24" | zone 4, moist, rich soil |

GROUND COVERS:  perennial

Ground covers are excellent soil and bank retainers as well as accent plants and borders. As a group, they are more drought tolerant than grass and some can even be walked on - an interesting  alternative to grass in small areas.  (See Perennials page 58**.)

NATURAL and INERT GROUND COVER:

DECORATIVE BARK: Bark is a very useful ground cover. It...
- Helps maintain moisture in the soil.
- Improves soil as it decomposes.
- Helps keep grass from encroaching in beds and tree wells.
- Provides weed control when used 3" deep.

It is okay in flower beds until your perennials grow together; thus, eliminating the need for bark. Soil Pep®/Mulch is also a nice decorative ground cover for flower beds and trees although it will decompose quicker.

Bark comes in four basic styles: Shredded, Small, Medium and Large nuggets.

Shredded bark is best for pathways, playgrounds and higher wind areas since it lays the flattest.

Small, Medium and Large nuggets are cosmetically attractive and can be used in flower beds, pathways, around trees and shrubs, etc.  Which kind you choose is a matter of personal preference and site needs.

WEED BARRIER: A porous fabric which allows water to penetrate but prevents weeds and other plants from growing through it. Can be used on pathways, play areas and other locations you wish to keep "weed free" for awhile. As the bark breaks down, seed can germinate on the organic matter and it will become necessary to redo the fabric.

Another use for weed barrier is in gardens and shrub beds. It helps maintain a handsome, weed free look while you are waiting for the plants to fill in. You can add plants to the bed by moving bark out of the way, slashing a large "X" and planting in the earth. The "X" must be large enough to accommodate plant growth.

Weed barrier can also be used for French Drains and in roof run-off areas to reduce "mud" splash on the foundation.

## ANNUALS

About annuals at elevation: Use cold-hardy varieties to fill in spaces between perennials in new gardens. Plant them very, very close together - maybe 6" apart or less. Try to limit tender annuals to containers that can be protected with frost cloth in case of the annual late June frost as it is quite painful to throw out slimy impatiens, marigolds, and geraniums and start over in the beginning of our summer!

Avoid greenhouse grown and raised stock - even cold-hardy varieties that have been "forced" to grow faster in a greenhouse need to be 'hardened off' outside before they are safe for you to plant outside at elevation. If you purchase a greenhouse grown plant (which is totally lush and irresistible), be prepared to cover it at night and protect it from wind, frost, and intense direct sunlight.

why did you even go there ~ L., K., CA, -what specific incident made you say that? Me-never- 
$-M, M, T.~ I wouldn't stay, yet it makes me think twice to even start!) why - letting go of my m? - my value? 
You asked 1x @ if i hated to work on people ~ why w ethic is strong enough if that was true, they would never know it sometimes I'd be really down + I would have to fake cheeriness - it would bring me up (after an hour) if it was some I liked (you) way way ↓ if I didn't like them but these people I mostly cut out of my practice (∅A) what if I lost the ability to 68 cheer up - even fakely.

Here is a list of some of the Annuals available to our area, classified as:
THE BEST - meaning cold and frost tolerant; GOOD - meaning they can perform but
usually give up after a couple of light frosts and the first heavy frost; BAD but
BEAUTIFUL - intolerant to frost, high altitude sun, and wind.

| THE BEST: | GOOD: | BAD but BEAUTIFUL: |
|---|---|---|
| White buttons, | Alyssum, | Ageratum, |
| Dianthus, | Calendula, | Begonia,Celosia, |
| Dusty Miller, | Cleome, | Coleus, Dahlia, |
| Flowering Cabbage | Cosmos, | Impatiens, Marigold, |
| and Kale, | Gazania, | Morning glory, Salvia, |
| Pansy, Petunia, | Sunflowers, | Zinnia, Fuchsia, New |
| Gaura, Snapdragons, | Lisianthus, | Guinea Impatiens, |
| Stocks, Viola, | Lobelia, | Bougainvillea, |
| **"Proven Winners®"** | Nasturtium, | anything tropical and lush |
| Bacopa, Cuphea, | Nemesia, | |
| Carnation, Cobbity | Nierembergia, | ❀ DON'T expect these varieties to gain |
| Daisy, Diascia, | annual Penstemon, | much size  here during the summer. |
| Gypsophila, | Poppy, | |
| Helichrysum, | Portulaca, Ivy, | |
| Linaria, Lotus Vine, | Fountain grass | |
| Million Bells, Sage, | | |
| Scaevola, Verbena, | | |
| Dracena, Sweet | | |
| Annie, Borage | | |

❀ Many of these varieties
are used in European
Window Boxes.

# SHADE TOLERANT PLANTS

Here is a reference to some of the varieties we have found which can tolerate different amounts of shade - from deep shade to partial shade.

Shade is not an abundant commodity here, but many people have exposures that receive minimal sun due to structures or plants. The more trees you plant, the more shade you will have in the future.

## FLOWERS:

| | |
|---|---|
| Ajuga | Lady's Mantle |
| Basket of Gold | Lamiastrum |
| Beacon Silver | Leopard's Bane |
| Bee Balm - *Monarda* | Hosta Lily |
| Bishop's Weed | Lily of the Valley |
| Bleeding Heart | Lovage |
| Blue Bells | Lupin |
| Campanula | Mallow |
| Clematis | Meadowsweet |
| Columbine | Monkshood |
| Coral Bells | Moss |
| Cranesbill Geranium | Obedient Plant |
| Creeping Jenny | Pachysandra |
| Daylily | Purple Palace - *Heuchera* |
| False Spirea - *Astilbe* | Primrose |
| Foam Flower | Sandwort |
| Forget-me-nots | Saxifraga - *Bergenia* |
| Foxglove | Silvermound |
| Fragaria | Spiderwort |
| Globeflower - *Trollius* | Sweet Woodruff |
| Jacob's Ladder | Thyme -Assorted varieties |

# TREES AND SHRUBS THAT CAN TOLERATE SHADE:

◗ ✹ Alpine Fir

◗ White Fir

✹ ● Amur Maple

◗● ● Dwarf Burning Bush

✹ ● Red-Twig Dogwood

◗● ● Variegated Red-Twig Dogwood

◗● ● Yellow Twig Dogwood

◗ Hawthorn

◗ ● Dwarf Alberta Spruce

✹ ● Juniper varieties

◗● Scarlet 'Dropmore' Honeysuckle

◗● ● Siberian Cypress

● Snowberry

✹ ● Spruce

◗● ● Swedish Aspen

◗ Mountain Ash

✹ Full Sun

● Full Shade

◗ Partial Sun

◗ Root Shade

71

# PLANTS THAT OFFER FALL COLOR or INTEREST:

Sometimes we forget to plant fall color into our yards because they are not "showing off" for us while we are purchasing plants during the summer months.

Here is a list of Trees, Shrubs, and Flowers that will get your attention in the fall and carry you through the October snow showers into winter dormancy:

## TREES

| Variety | Description |
|---|---|
| Aspen | bright yellow leaves to red-orange |
| Swedish Aspen | red-orange leaves, needs slightly protected site |
| Mountain Ash | red-orange leaves, bright berry, needs protected site |
| American Mtn. Ash | red-orange leaves, reddish berry, needs protection |
| Western Red Birch | yellow leaves, reddish brown bark in winter |
| Lanceleaf Cottonwood | yellow leaves, whitish-gray trunk in winter |
| Flowering Crabapple | see Flowering Crab List also page 40 |
|     Brandywine | reddish/orange leaves |
|     Bechtel | 'orangish' |
|     Royalty | purple |
|     Hopa | pretty red berries |
|     Dolgo | delicious, edible red berries |
|     Radiant | bronzy leaves, bright red berries |
|     Sugar Tyme | yellow leaves, persistent red berries |
| Canada Redcherry | purple leaves, constant color throughout season! |
| Evergreens | green, texture and constant color throughout seasons |
| Honeylocust | honey-yellow, needs a protected site |
| Golden Willow | yellow leaves, bright yellow branches all year |
| Amur Maple | brilliant red fall color, clumping or tree form |
| Autumn Blaze Maple | red fall color, needs some protection from direct wind |

## SHRUBS WITH FALL INTEREST

| Variety | Description |
|---|---|
| Ashleaf Spirea | red-bronze leaf, nice dried flower plume |
| Barberry | red-purple fall color, needs protected site |
| Burning Bush | flame red fall color, needs protected site |
| Common Chokecherry | reddish/orange leaves, edible fruit |
| Schubert Chokecherry | purple/red leaves, occasional berry |
| Peking Cotoneaster | red-orange leaves, dark black berry |
| Golden Currant | reddish leaves, edible golden berry |
| Redtwig Dogwood | red leaves, red stem throughout the winter |
| Variegated Redtwig Dogwood | red, variegated leaf, red stem through winter |
| Yellowtwig Dogwood | yellow stem throughout the winter |
| Evergreens | constant green through all seasons |
| Amur Maple | brilliant red leaves, large shrub/small tree |
| Mahonia repens | red-purple foliage, purple berries |
| Redleaf Rose | red leaves, medium sized rose hips |
| Rugosa Rose | yellow leaves, large red rose hips |
| Woods Rose | yellow leaves, profuse red rose hips |
| Sagebrush | silvery-gray foliage, golden, feathery seed heads |
| Serviceberry | yellow leaves, edible purple berry |
| Snowberry | insignificant leaf, profuse white berries through winter |
| Spirea 'Anthony Waterer' | burgundy leaf, nice dried flower |
| Three Leaf Sumac | red-orange lobed leaf |
| Staghorn Sumac | reddish leaves, great texture |
| Assorted Viburnum | yellow-red leaves, wonderful berries |

*Viburnum*

## FLOWERS for FALL:  (Also see Perennials by Bloom Time page 64 )

| Variety | Description |
|---|---|
| Artemisia | silvery foliage |
| Fall blooming Asters | reds to purples, hardy mounding plants |
| Baby's breath | white to pink dried flowers |
| Coneflowers | purple, white and yellow hardy, daisy-like perennials |
| Daylily | assorted colors, leafy, grass-like foliage |
| Euphorbia | orangish foliage, early and late interest! |
| Gaillardia | yellow, orange, burgundy late daisy bloomers |
| Lamb's Ear | soft, silver foliage, pinkish bloom |
| Monarda | pinks to reds, late bloomer |
| Mums | Garden mums assorted colors, tender perennial |
| Pansy | best when planted in spring-summer-all colors |
| Tall Garden Phlox | assorted colors, fragrant |
| Sedum Autumn Joy | red-pink, upright variety |
| Dragon's Blood | red foliage and bloom |
| Tri-Color | red-pink variegated foliage, pink flower |
| Vera Jameson | purplish foliage, mauve flower |

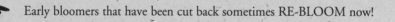 Early bloomers that have been cut back sometimes RE-BLOOM now!

*Purple Coneflower*

## HERBS:

Herbs are an interesting addition to perennial gardens and annual planters. They add that extra appeal of usefulness and flavor to your pots and baskets. Clip some chives from your perennial patch for your potatoes and cottage cheese or add a sprig of dill out of your flower pot for flavor.

## PERENNIAL HERBS FOR GARDENS AND CONTAINERS

| VARIETY | | USES/DESCRIPTION |
|---|---|---|
| Lady's Mantle | 4-6" | medicinal for "ladies" herb |
| Burnet | 24" | salads, cold drinks, herb vinegars and cream cheese |
| Babys Breath | 24" | pretty filler for bouquets |
| Chamomile | 4" | white daisy flower on soft green foliage, tea, calming, and relaxing. |
| Chives | 8-20" | delicate onion flavor |
| Comfrey | 30" | medicinal, "Bone Set", self-seeding |
| Curry | 36" | tender perennial, nice accent; meat dishes |
| Bee Balm | 18-30" | attracts bees, butterflies, hummingbirds; *'Monarda'* |
| Echinacea | 24" | primary constituent in historical medicine |
| Elephant Garlic | 30" | mild and larger than regular garlic |
| Feverfew | 24" | medicinal for headaches; *'Matricaria'* |
| Flax | 18" | seed contains acids necessary for bodily functions |
| French Tarragon | 8" | use in soups and meat dishes |
| Garlic | 12" | medicinal, world-wide favorite for immune system |
| Garlic Chives | 8-20" | larger variety than regular chives |
| Hops | Vine | used in beer |
| Horseradish | 12" | plant as a root, very strong flavor |
| Lemon Balm | 12" | medicinal; lemon-mint flavor, soup and salad |
| Lovage | 60" | leaves have celery flavor |
| Oregano | 24" | leaves used for Italian dishes |

PERENIAL HERBS:  for garden and container growing.

| VARIETY | | USES/DESCRIPTION |
|---|---|---|
| Greek Oregano | 24" | italian seasoning; grows in a mound |
| Lamb's Ear | 12" | medicinal, soft silver foliage, contrast plant |
| Lavender-Munstead | 12" | medicinal, used in aromatherapy |
| Mints: | (aggressive) | varieties: Applemint, Bergamot, Catmint, Chocolate, Orangemint, Spearmint |
| Sage | | species include Tri-color, common, etc. |
| Thyme | | varieties: Cat, Creeping, English, Lemon, Mother-of, Woolly; Great for cooking |

☞ *BE CAREFUL, many herbs considered perennial elsewhere do not come back at our elevation, for example, Rosemary.

*Sage*

## ANNUAL HERBS at ELEVATION - For containers and yearly planting in herb gardens. Some are not frost tolerant.

| VARIETY | | USES/DESCRIPTION |
|---|---|---|
| Anise | 24" | medicinal; licorice flavored |
| Basils | 8" | many wonderful varieties; NO frost tolerance; great in all cooking |
| Borage | 24" | medicinal; very aggressive; salads and tea |
| Catnip | 30" | addictive for cats |
| Chamomile | 18" | medicinal for "calming" |
| Cilantro | 24" | good in salsa |
| Dill | 36" | Fernleaf variety; fish, chicken, bread |
| Fennel | 48" | medicinal for digestion; licorice flavored leaves |
| Gopher Purge | 60" | biennial, roots poisonous to gophers |
| Lavender-French | 12-18" | tender perennial; lovely aroma for sachets |
| Lemon Verbena | 60" | tender perennial; strong lemon scent |
| Marigold(Calendula) | 18-24" | medicinal(antiseptic), deters bugs in garden |
| Marjoram | 18" | soup, salad dressing, eggs, lamb |
| Italian Parsley | 18" | biennial; stronger flavor than curled |
| Triple-curl Parsley | 18" | biennial; garnish and seasoning |
| Chervill | 24" | gourmet parsley |
| Corsican Mint | 2' | very strong mint used in créme de menthe |
| Pineapple Mint | 18" | fragrant |
| Rosemary | 36" | *Officinalis*; Italian seasoning, upright habit |
| Rosemary | 6-12" | *Prostratus*; trailing habit |
| Rue | 24" | bitter tonic, good insect guard in garden |
| Pineapple Sage | 30" | tender perennial; salads, herb butter |
| Tri-color Sage | 24" | tender perennial; purple/white/green |
| Savory | 18" | salads, meats, soups |
| St. John's Wort | 12" | medicinal for nerves; yellow flower |
| Sweet Annie | 3-5' | very aggressive, fragrant, good for wreaths |
| Wormwood | 18" | medicinal for parasitic expulsion |

*Italian Parsley*

## BULBS:

Bulbs are the long awaited welcome to spring. They bloom in late April, May and June. Be sure to save space for them in your perennial gardens and around some of your trees.

Hardy spring blooming bulbs need to be planted in the fall of the previous season. When you see them blooming in the spring, it's too early to plant them (or too late!). Mark your calendar to buy bulbs in September/October. The best varieties for performance in the mountains are:

- Crocus
- Grape Hyacinths, Snow drops, Dutch Iris
- Daffodils
- Narcissus
- Tulips - Rock garden, Darwin, Triumph, Parrot, Lily-Flowering

Planting bulbs at this elevation is different from other climates. ONLY plant them down 2 1/2 times the width of the bulb; NEVER any deeper or they may not come up. The soil is heavy and spring does not warm the ground quickly enough to encourage them.

Plant bulbs "tips up"     Larger bulbs - 5 bulbs per square foot
                          Smaller bulbs and corms 10-15 per square foot

☛ If you know you have a rodent problem, plant bulbs inside a chicken wire box. This can discourage them considerably.

☛ If your bulbs have a little bit of fungus or mold on them, lightly dust them with Soil Sulphur.

Plant bulbs in groups of 5 or more. It is far better to have a small area with a blast of color than try to spread a few bulbs over a large area.

As your bulbs are beginning to come up and bloom in the spring, sprinkle some bonemeal, blood meal, super-triple-phosphate, or all purpose fertilizer at the base of the plants.

Enjoy your blossoms. If you are using them as cut flowers, cut only the flower. Leave the leaves on the plant and allow them to die completely back to the ground before cutting them off. If the look of the dying leaves bothers you, you may band them together until they are dry and crispy. Then, and only then, should you cut them off. The dying leaves send energy back to the bulb for next years bloom!

Narcissus, Daffodil, and crocus continue to grow in this climate. They can eventually be divided and are naturally drought tolerant which lends them to being naturalized - planted in areas which receive minimal water.

Tulips, the showy, colorful species, only perform well in this climate. They do not increase in size. Consequently, they need to be re-planted every three to five years as their color and size diminishes. It is best to start with the biggest bulbs you can possibly find.

You will notice, the first few years after planting, tulips are spectacular. After awhile, they become smaller and smaller. Tulip patches need to be "beefed up" every three to five years. Take photos of bulb areas while they are in bloom so you know where they are. Maybe mark areas with a stick or string, anything to indicate where you need to supplemental plant in the fall.

Choosing bulbs is easy. . . Large and Firm. If you can physically purchase your bulbs at a retail nursery, the quality of the bulbs will be better. You get what you pay for and can feel for yourself. Mail Order tends to arrive at elevation past the first snow fall so you either don't get them in the ground or you are digging in snow and muck to plant them - plus, it is very easy to buy what looks pretty in a catalog and end up with inferior quality bulbs (smaller and less fresh), and varieties that don't perform at elevation.

## SUMMER BLOOMING BULBS and CORMS:

Plant in spring for possible late summer color. These are not extremely successful due to the early frosts and short growing season. Anemones (Windflower) do fairly well, Gladiolas usually do not have time to bloom before the frost but have been seen blooming here - be prepared to cover with frost cloth. Begonias, Dahlias and the rest. . . Buy the plant!

## FALL BLOOMING BULBS:

Plant in the fall with spring blooming bulbs. They are usually blooming right out of the box at the garden center. They can be a little pricey but add a very unusual interest to the fall garden. Hardy too. Assorted Fall-blooming Crocus - Speciosus, Sativus, Kotschyanus.

## TUBEROUS ROOTS:

Tuberous roots can be planted in spring or fall in the root form or throughout the summer from an established container. They include

- Daylily
- Bleeding Heart
- Peony
- Iris
- Asiatic Lily - planted deeper than other roots.

PLANTING TUBEROUS ROOTS - Differs by variety but, in general

1) Dig hole in amended soil large enough to contain root.

2) Spread roots out in hole.

3) For Daylily and Iris, place root shallow enough so that the green top is just above ground.

3) For Peony, make sure tuber is just below soil surface with eyes peeking at ground level.

4) Fill in with soil, eliminate all air pockets, fertilize with bone meal, and water well.

*Iris Pod*

# ROSES:

"Do you have any Roses?" A question frequently asked at the nursery. . . Yes, some roses do "floribunda" at elevation, but most hybrid tea roses cannot thrive through all of our winters. With special care they can survive, but we've found they don't perform as well as they can. They may even do well for several seasons and then we'll have an unseasonably cold, dry fall or spring (no snow pack for insulation) and that does them in. . . you have to start all over again.

Rugosa Roses, some Heirloom and Shrub Roses do fairly well. If they can be kept out of really windy sites, they do even better. Following is a list of some varieties we've found that seem to "winter well" at altitude.

## RUGOSA
### * Proven performers

| Zone | Variety | Height | Description | Bloom |
|------|---------|--------|-------------|-------|
| 3 | Adelaide Hoodless | 3' | Double bright red | Repeat |
| 3 | Agnes* | 4-6' | Double yellow, fragrant | Continuous |
| 4 | Blanc Double de Coubert | 5-7' | Double white, fragrant | Continuous |
| 4 | Grootendorst* | 3-4' | Pink | Summer |
| 3 | FJ Grootendorst* | 4-6' | Double crimson red | Repeat |
| 3 | Hansa* | 4-5' | Red-violet, large hips | Summer |
| 3 | Harrison's Yellow* | 4-6' | Dbl yellow, arching cane | Early Summer |
| 3 | Linda Campbell | 4-6' | Dbl velvety bright red | Repeat |
| 3 | Sir Thomas Lipton | 6-8' | Dbl white, fragrant | Repeat |
| 3 | Theresa Bugnet* | 4-6' | Lilac buds open pink | Summer |
| 4 | Topaz Jewel | 4-5' | Butter cream yellow | Repeat |

# SHRUB AND HEIRLOOM ROSES

* Proven performers

| Zone | Variety | Height | Description | Bloom |
|------|---------|--------|-------------|-------|
| 3 | Austrian Copper* | 6' | brilliant copper-red | late spring |
| 3 | Baby Blanket | 3x5' | light pink | long bloom |
| 3 | Fairy Polyanthe | 3-4' | pastel pink clusters | repeat |
| 4 | Gourmet Popcorn | 3-5' | abundant white, miniature | continuous fragrant |
| 3 | Morden Blush* | 3' | light pink | repeat |
| 3 | Morden Centennial* | 3-4' | pink single clusters | repeat |
| 4 | Nearly Wild | 2-3' | floribunda clusters single rose, pink | repeat |
| 3 | Oranges and Lemons | 6' | orange stripe yellow new foliage yellow | repeat |
| 3 | Prairie Joy | 4-5' | pink | summer |
| 3 | Persian Yellow* | 4-6' | double bright yellow | early summer |
| 4 | Rosa Hugonis | 4-6' | Father Hugo-single yellow | spring |
| 2 | Rosa Rubrifolia* | 5-6' | pink, red foliage orange-red hips | mid summer |
| 2 | Rosa Rugosa Rubra* | 6' | large single mauve orange-red hips | repeat |
| 4 | Rosa Woodsii* | 4-5' | pale pink, native to intermountain | summer |

# MEIDILAND

*Proven Performers

| Zone | Variety | Height - Description | Bloom |
|------|---------|---------------------|-------|
| 4 | Bonica | 3'  pink; compact | everblooming |
| 3 | Pink Meidiland* | 2-3'  deep pink/white eye | repeat |
| 3 | Red Meidiland* | spreading  red/white eye | repeat |
| 3 | Scarlet Meidiland* | 3'  bright cherry red | mid-late |
| 3 | White Meidiland* | 3-4'  spreading, pure white | repeat |

# CLIMBING ROSES

| Zone | Variety | Height - Description |
|------|---------|---------------------|
| 5 | Don Juan Climber | 10  dark red |
| 4 | Dortmund | 8-10'  single red with white eye, red hips, blooms on old and new canes |
| 3 | Henry Kelsey | 6'  double rose, repeat bloomer; spicy fragrance |
| 4 | New Dawn | 18'  white; blush pink |
| 4 | Seven Sisters | 10'  pale rose to crimson cascades |
| 3 | William Baffin | 7-9'  double pink, repeat bloomer, good disease resistance |

> Roses don't usually reach their full height at elevation due to the short growing season 👈

## FRUIT:

Mountainous regions are not the center of agricultural, commercial fruit production, but there is a little bit of harvesting you can do in your own yard.

(See 'Birdscaping' page 43 for more edible fruit.)

| BERRIES | | FRUITING HABIT | ZONE |
|---|---|---|---|
| **Blackberry:** | | | |
| Black Satin | -10 | thornless, large and firm | 4 |
| Hull | -10 | thornless, large and juicy | 4 |
| **Currant:** | | | |
| Crandall Black | -30 | high yield, large fruit | 3 |
| Golden | -30 | very hardy, golden | 3 |
| Red Lake | -30 | large, red | 3 |
| **Gooseberry:** | | | |
| Champion | -35 | green fruit | 3 |
| Orus | -35 | dark purple | 3 |
| Pixwell | -35 | dark pink | 3 |
| **Raspberry:** | | | |
| Red Canby | -30 | early, thornless, large and firm | 3 |
| Heritage | hardy | summer/fall; small and dry | 4 |
| Red Latham | -30 | mid-season | 4 |
| **Rhubarb:** | | | |
| Canada Red | hardy | red stalks throughout | 3 |
| **Strawberry:** | | | |
| All-Star | hardy | June/July bearing | 4 |
| Fort Laramie | hardy | everbearing | 4 |

# FRUIT TREES:

APPLES - standard and semi-dwarf varieties; 20'x20' average. Generally not self-fertile. Use two different varieties that bloom at approximately the same time. Plant within 100' of the pollinator. Hardier choices are *.

| VARIETY | DESCRIPTION | ZONE |
|---|---|---|
| *Beacon | standard, summer, juicy bright red fruit, hardy, heavy bearing, excellent eating | 3 |
| Golden Delicious | mid-season to late, clear yellow fruit, highly aromatic; crisp, eating/cooking | 5 |
| Red Delicious | mid-season to late, color varies with strain and garden climate | 5 |
| *Haralson | semi-dwarf, winter, medium size, bright red, tart, juicy, crisp, often bears fruit the first year | 3 |
| Jonathon | fall-winter, medium size, round, bright red, sweet flesh, crisp and juicy; dessert/cooking | 5 |
| *MacIntosh | mid-season, large, bright red with tart, snow white fruit; stores well | 3 |
| *Mantet | standard, summer, medium red apple, skin is yellow striped and blushed with red, juicy, sweet fruit | 3 |
| *Red Baron | standard, fall, very hardy, medium to large, juicy flesh, good for eating/pies | 3 |
| *Red Duchess | standard, very hardy, summer, medium to large, juicy apple | 4 |
| *Yellow Transparent | summer, medium greenish yellow, white juicy flesh, excellent for pies, scab resistant | 4 |
| *Wealthy | small, cold-hardy tree that tends to alternate bearing years, large rough red fruit, flesh veined pink, firm/tart/juicy | 4 |
| Italian Plum | medium size, sweet, purplish-black, late mid-season, do NOT plant by raspberry, potatoes, strawberry, tomatoes | 4 |

WILDFLOWERS: Following is a list of wildflower seed available to purchase. There are native and introduced varieties, all wonderful performers in the right location. Some native varieties are inaccessible at the retail level. Many varieties are also available in the plant form in containers.

Seed should not be harvested from the mountains because of the delicate balance of nature. Enjoy but don't harvest.

## WILDFLOWER SEED VARIETIES AND CHARACTERISTICS

### Perennials

| COMMON NAME | SCIENTIFIC NAME | HEIGHT | COLOR | SUN | BLOOM |
|---|---|---|---|---|---|
| Arrowleaf Balsamroot | *Balsamorhisa* | 16-30" | yellow | sun | early |
| Wild Bergamot | *Monarda fistulosa* | 12-36" | pink | sun/pt. shade | early |
| Pacific Aster | *Aster chilensis* | 8-12" | lavender | sun | early-mid |
| Black-eyed Susan | *Rudbeckia hirta* | 18-48" | lavender | sun | early-mid |
| Blanket Flower | *Gaillardia aristata* | 18-24" | yellow/orange | sun | mid/late |
| Blue Flax | *Linum lewisii* | 24" | blue | sun | early-late |
| Colorado Columbine | *Aquilegia coerulea* | 12-30" | blue | shade/pt. sun | early |
| Coneflower, Prairie | *Ratibida columnaris* | 12-24" | yellow | sun | mid |
| Coneflower, Purple | *Echinacea purpurea* | 24-36" | purple | sun/pt. shade | late |
| Lanceleaf Coreopsis | *Coreopsis lanceolata* | 12-24" | yellow | part shade | mid |
| Daisy, Aspen | *Erigeron speciosus* | 12-24" | lavender/white | sun/pt. shade | mid |
| Daisy, Ox-eye | *Chrysanthemum leucanthe* | 24-48" | white | sun/pt. shade | mid |
| Daisy, Shasta | *Chrysanthemum maximum* | 24-36" | white | sun | mid |
| Dame's Rocket | *Hesperis matronalis* | 24-48" | lavender | part shade | mid |
| Fireflower | *Epilobium angustifolium* | 14-84" | hot pink | sun | mid-late |
| Wild Geranium | *Geranium viscosissimum* | 12-48" | pink/lavender | diffused | early |
| Desert Globemallow | *Spaeralcea* | 20-38" | orange/red | sun | mid-late |
| Golden Banner | *Thermopsis montanus* | 12-48" | yellow | part shade | mid |
| Rocky Mountain Iris | *Iris missouriensis* | 8-20" | blue | sun | early |
| Maiden Pinks | *Dianthus deltoides* | 12-18" | pink/red | sun | mid |
| Red Mexican Hat | *Ratibida ssp. forma* | 12-24" | red | sun | mid |
| Mountain Lupine | *Lupinus alpestris* | 12-20" | blue/lavender | shade/sun | early |
| Indian Paintbrush | *Castilleja chromosa* | 4-18" | red/orange | sun | mid |

| COMMON NAME | SCIENTIFIC NAME | HEIGHT | COLOR | SUN | BLOOM |
|---|---|---|---|---|---|
| Large Flowered Penstemon | *Penstemon grandiflora* | 24-48" | pink/white | shade | mid |
| Rocky Mountain Penstemon | *Penstemon strictus* | 12-36" | violet | shade/sun | early-mid |
| Wasatch Penstemon | *Penstemon cyananthus* | 18" | blue | part shade | early-mid |
| Iceland Poppy | *Papaver nudicule* | 24" | yellow/orange | sun | mid |
| White Evening Primrose | *Oenothera ssp.* | 8-20" | white/lavender | sun | early-mid |
| Showy Goldeneye | *Viguiera multiflora* | 12-40" | yellow | part shads | late |
| Sulfur Flower | *Eriogonum umbellatum* | 6-12" | yellow | sun/pt. shade | late |
| Northern Sweetvetch | *Hedysarum boreale* | 10-24" | pink/purple | part shade | mid |
| Yarrow, Golden | *Achillea fillipendula* | 36-48" | yellow | sun | mid-late |
| Yarrow, White | *Achillea millefolium* | 12-24" | white | sun | mid-late |

## Annuals

| COMMON NAME | SCIENTIFIC NAME | HEIGHT | COLOR | SUN | BLOOM |
|---|---|---|---|---|---|
| Baby Blue Eyes | *Nemophila menziesii* | 6-10" | blue | shade | mid-late |
| Bachelor Button | *Centaurea cyanus* | 8-30" | blue | sun/shade | mid-late |
| Chinese Houses | *Collinsea heterophylla* | 24" | lavender/white | shade | mid-late |
| Plains Coreopsis | *Coreopsis tinctoria* | 24-48" | yellow/burgundy | part shade | mid-late |
| Cosmos | *Cosmos bipinnatus* | 30-48" | pink | sun | mid-late |
| Farewell to Spring | *Clarkia amoena* | 6-36" | pink and red | part shade | mid-late |
| Scarlet Flax | *Linum grandiflorum rubrum* | 14" | scarlet/red | part shade | mid-late |
| Globegilia | *Gilia capitata* | 12-24" | blue | part shade | mid-late |
| Rocket Larkspur | *Delphinium ajacis* | 12-36" | white/pink/blue | part shade | mid-late |
| Drummond Phlox | *Phlox drummondii* | 8-20" | red/mix | sun | mid-late |
| Poppy, California | *Eschscholtzia california* | 12-18" | orange | sun | mid-late |
| Poppy, Flanders | *Papaver rhoeas* | 24" | red | sun/part shade | mid-late |
| Poppy, Shirley's | *Papaver rhoeas* | 24" | pastels | sun/part shade | mid-late |
| Rocky Mountain Bee Plant | *Cleome serrulata* | 12-48" | pink/purple | sun | mid-late |
| Baby Snapdragon | *Linaria maroccana* | 18-24" | mixed | sun/part shade | mid-late |
| Annual sunflower | *Helianthus* | 36-72" | yellow | sun | mid-late |
| Tidy Tips | *Layia platyglossa* | 6-12" | yellow & white | sun | mid-late |
| Wallflower | *Chieranthus allionii* | 12-18" | orange | sun | mid-late |

GRASSES: Following is a list of recommended grass varieties available in seed form for our elevation. Other varieties can be purchased depending on your specific vegetation and re-vegetation needs.

| VARIETY | SCIENTIFIC NAME | HEIGHT |
|---------|-----------------|--------|
| Crested Wheatgrass | *Agropyron cristatum* | 13-24" |
| Pubescent Wheatgrass | *Agropyron trichophourum* | 13-24" |
| Tall Wheatgrass | *Agropyron elongatum* | 25"+ |
| Intermediate Wheatgrass | *Agropyron intermedium* | 13-24" |
| Streambank Wheatgrass | *Agropyron riparium* | 6-24" |
| Western Wheatgrass | *Pascopyrum smithii* | 13-24" |
| Smooth Brome | *Bromus inermis* | 13-24" |
| Mountain Brome | *Bromus marginatus* | 25"+ |
| Orchardgrass | *Dactylis glomerata* | 18-25" |
| Tall Fescue | *Festuca arundinacea* | 25"+ |
| Hard Fescue | *Festuca longifolia* (turf) | 13-24" |
| Sheep Fescue | *Festuca ovina* | 13-24" |
| Annual Ryegrass | *Lolium multiflorum* | 25" |
| Perennial Ryegrass | *Lolium perenne* (turf) | 13-25" |
| Alpine Bluegrass | *Poa alpina* | 1-12" |
| Canada Bluegrass | *Poa compressa* | 13-24" |
| Kentucky Bluegrass | *Poa pratensis* (turf) | 13-24" |

## BLENDS

| VARIETY | DESCRIPTION | HEIGHT |
|---------|-------------|--------|
| Park City Premium Lawn Blend® | Bluegrass Blend for elevation | 13-24" |
| Low Maintenance Lawn Blend | Mix of drought tolerant seed | 13-24" |
| Dryland Pasture Blend | Edible blend for dryland grazing | 2-24" |
| Wetland Pasture Blend | Edible blend for wetland grazing | 6-24" |

## VEGETABLES:

Vegetables are somewhat tricky at elevation but there are a lot of dedicated gardeners growing a fair share of cold-hardy crops including gourmet lettuces, herbs, heirloom vegetables, carrots, spinach and potatoes - from russets to all blue.

REMEMBER, every season at elevation is different. Do not expect the same results by the calendar.

Soil is essential. It needs to be "rich and loose." To prepare the soil initially add fresh topsoil and compost.

Alternating seasons, plant a cover crop of vetch, clover or alfalfa. Turn this "green" plant into your garden in the fall or spring as a green manure. (Essential to growing quality veggies year after year!)

Crop rotation also helps keep your soil healthy. Plant a different family of vegetable in each area annually, i.e. corn one season, potatoes the next, lettuce the next, etc.

During the growing season, keep in mind that if there is a threat of frost, cover your garden. Seedlings cannot tolerate frost. Tender varieties like tomatoes, peppers, squash, cucumbers, pumpkins and corn cannot tolerate frost. Invest in a good frost cover for your garden. "Harden off" your seedlings before setting them out for a full night.

## WATERING VEGETABLES

Keep your soil consistently moist but not soaked or too dry.  Vegetables are extremely sensitive to irregular watering habits.  Try to water before 9 a.m. or between 5 and 7 p.m.

If you are trying to grow from seed, the following vegetables should be started indoors no later than March 1.  Plant in garden after last frost date – between June 15 and July 5.

- Tomatoes
- Peppers
- Squash
- Cucumbers
- Corn
- Pumpkins

These plants will never be frost tolerant.  Cover whenever there is the slightest threat of frost.

Broccoli can also be started inside or outside after the soil reaches 45°.  Starts are preferable.

As soon as the soil is relatively dry, workable, and has warmed to the recommended temperature, plant:

- Lettuces   50°
- Spinach   50°
- Peas        50°
- Radishes   40°
- Chard      60°
- Potatoes
- Beets- moderate growth until temperatures  stay in the 60's
- Carrots – excellent frost tolerance
- Leeks – have good frost tolerance
- Onions – have good frost tolerance
- Other root crops

Garlic can be planted in spring or fall.  Asparagus should be planted in the spring.

Tip:  When purchasing seeds, pick varieties with good frost tolerance and a short growing season.  Look for Heirloom and open pollinated varieties.

*what, when, where, why bother?*

*"An onion can make people cry, but there's no
Vegetable that can make them laugh."*

Anonymous

# chapter III: WHEN TO. . .

*"You observe a lot by watching."*

-Coach Berra

3

chapter III: WHEN TO...

**April**   Start garden and yard clean-ups on nice days

**May**   Do preventative treatments; fertilize; start your tree and shrub planting

**Remember, at elevation, you can plant from spring through fall.**

*"I wonder what it would be like to live in a world where it was always June?"* - L.M. Montgomery

**June**   Plant container gardens

**July**   Fertilize lightly; plant and enjoy summer

**August**   *"Summer's lease has all too short a date."*
                        -William Shakespeare

**September/October:** Plant bulbs; winterize lawn and garden; spray anti-desiccant on evergreens; spread vole repellent and fungicide for lawn. Crabgrass pre-emergent can be laid down now for spring. Get in the spirit of the season with pumpkins, dried flowers and seasonal wreaths.

**November/December**   Plant Paperwhites for Christmas. Force bulbs indoors for winter color... Get your skis ready!

## WHEN TO...

Patience is the key to mountain gardening. Spring is a long, drawn out season intermingled with sunny days and snow showers, many hard frosts, and a few of those "perfect days." It basically lasts from March until June.

PLANT SEED: Wildflower seed and mixes can be planted anytime from early spring through June and still bloom in late June and July.

Perennial seed can be sown anytime throughout the year. Seed can germinate with temperatures between 65 degrees and 85 degrees. Any cooler or hotter temperatures put the seed into a heat or cold induced dormancy where it lies until the length of the day and germination temperatures are ideal - sometimes it will stay there until the following season.

Annual seed can be planted in late fall or spring (before the middle of June) for germination and blooming during that season. If it is planted later than June 15, it may germinate but probably will not have time to flower that season. If it is planted before late fall, it may germinate and then freeze before it has time to flower. It can be good for a wildflower patch that has been planted late to have annuals coming up even if they don't bloom because they take up space where weeds could invade.

WHEN TO PLANT GRASS SEED: When planting grassy areas that will not be irrigated (fields and native areas), it is best to seed in the fall. That way the seed can absorb moisture all winter and take advantage of spring rain to encourage germination as soon as the days get long enough and the ground heats up.

Any time you can supply supplemental water to a seeded area during the first growing season, it will benefit the new plants by creating a sturdier, healthier root system. Recognizing of course that at times this is impossible, any extra water does help.

For lawn and irrigated areas, grass seed can be planted from early spring through September 15-25, depending on the weather. Most grass seed varieties can germinate throughout the summer at this elevation. In the peak, heat week of August, some varieties may go into a heat induced dormancy and not germinate until the temperature drops back down into the 65-85 degree range.

See how to: Plant Wildflower Seed for watering specifics page 13.

WHEN TO PLANT TREES and SHRUBS: Mountain gardening is conducive to planting throughout the growing season. You can plant as long as the ground is soft enough to dig in. There is no better or worse season to plant. Each person has his or her own opinion and success story.

 If it works for you, carry on. . .

Some people like to plant in spring because the plant has a chance to become established throughout the growing season and goes into fall/winter as a semi-established plant.

Many people like fall planting because the plants are dormant and then, first thing in spring, before they can actually dig, the ground warms up enough for the roots to begin to develop.

If you have time and you feel like planting something - GO AHEAD AND GET IT IN THE GROUND no matter the season. A caution for mid-summer planting is to have your holes ready so the root ball and roots are not exposed to the sun very long!

**WHEN TO PLANT PERENNIALS:** Perennials can go in the ground anytime you can dig in your garden. When choosing plants, pick ones with a root system - flowers are nice, but a flower without a plant and root system is just a bloom. If you buy a plant with a flower, enjoy it for a few days then pinch it off and let the energy go to the leaves. The object the first season is to get a healthy plant and roots established.

One good reason to plant throughout the growing season is plant availability. Different plants are available at different times throughout the year. Not all varieties will be in stock on the day you decide to plant- that's nature's way.

**WHEN TO PLANT GROUND COVERS:** Ground covers can be planted anytime May through October. When using pony packs, it is better to plant in spring after the major frost heaves are finished so the plants don't pop out of the ground. If the plants do come out, it is usually safe to put them back in the ground - as long as the roots have not dried out.

## WHEN TO FERTILIZE

Fertilizing is not considered by most people an exciting topic, yet it is essential to exciting gardens and yards.

Living in an environment like ours, with poor, rocky, alkaline soil, lack of humidity and a short growing season, regular fertilization will increase plant growth and help maintain healthier lawns and yards. The stronger you keep your plants, the better they will be able to withstand unforeseen droughts, particularly cruel winters and unexpected seasonal killing frosts.

Next to proper soil preparation and proper plant selection, fertilizing is the most important aspect to maintaining a healthy landscape.

Seasonal fertilizing is a good way to break down the year:

WINTER: Take this season off, you deserve the break and so do your plants.

SPRING - April, May, early June: During the 'pre-emergent' time in spring, if you noticed you had a crabgrass and/or spurge problem with your lawn last year, an early spring application of crabgrass and spurge killer will help reduce this problem. It must be applied before you actually see the weeds or it is too late and you will need to resort to a post-emergence herbicide.

Spring is an excellent time to apply granular fertilizer like Morgro® Multi-purpose 16*16*8 plus Iron or Milorganite®. The ground moisture will help carry the nutrients into the roots.

Any established evergreens that yellowed severely over the winter can be treated with Chelated Iron in the Spring.

From May through September, every 4-6 weeks is a great time to use Morgro® Rootstarter or other root stimulants to promote root growth in newly planted plants, (1-2 years in the ground).

SUMMER - mid-June, July, August: Weed-&-Feed should be applied to your lawn if you have severe dandelion and clover problems. Try to apply before the weeds go to seed. Two applications may be necessary if weeds persist.

If your weed problem is limited, we recommend spot spraying with Morgro® "Weed-it-II" with Trimec®. It can be sprayed over grass and not damage it. Spot spraying is easy, effective, economical and better for the environment than general broadcasting or spraying.

You can and should use all-purpose fertilizer once or twice during the summer - depending on when your spring application was. Don't fertilize on the hottest day of the year. Try to make your applications on cooler days.

You can fertilize every 6-8 weeks.

Soil Acidifier, a liquid soil conditioner, can be used on lawns, trees, flower beds. It helps lower the pH of the soil which will create better growing conditions throughout the season, ultimately giving you healthier, stronger plants.

Soil Sulphur can also be applied throughout the summer to adjust soil pH.

FALL - September, October, November: 'Tis the season to plant bulbs and winterize your yard and gardens. Spray Wilt-pruf® on your spruce and evergreens to avoid needle desiccation over the winter.

When you fertilize in the fall, the fertilizer becomes available to the plant first thing in the spring - before you even think about your yard! If you like a green lawn early, fertilize in the fall.

It is also a good idea to broadcast granular fertilizer over your flower and shrub beds and in tree wells at this time.

Using mulch and/or a live compost as a protective layer over your gardens and around your trees and shrubs will not only protect them from frost without snow cover, but also improve your soil over the winter.

Although there are as many opinions regarding fertilizing as there are gardeners, the most important thing is

### REMEMBER TO FERTILIZE.

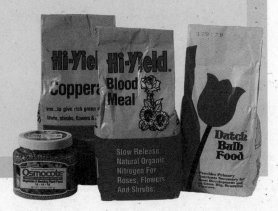

## WHEN TO: PRUNE

Nature does a pretty good job pruning here with snow pack, winter kill, and deer browsing, but there are a few guidelines to follow.

It is usually best to prune and shape in the spring. That way the plant has all summer to heal the wound. Plants usually heal fine without the aid of pruning paint and wraps in our dry climate. If it is necessary to dress a wound, use 1 Tablespoon of Clorox in a Cup of Water and apply to affected area. If the injury persists, pursue other avenues.

Dead limbs should be pruned before they rip healthy bark. This can be done at any time throughout the year. Cut your losses before they become worse.

Potentilla, Spirea and a few other varieties can be cut back in either the fall or the spring. They can handle a pretty serious clipping, even within a few inches of the ground if they are unruly.

Lilac and other flowering shrubs should be pruned after they bloom, before they set their buds for the following season.

When cutting, use sharp pruners, loppers, or handsaws. Make clean cuts at a 45 degree angle - don't force it, slice it.

Spoil yourself with great pruners - it makes the job easier.

## NOTES and IDEAS:
*what, when, where, why bother?*

# chapter IV: WHY BOTHER. . .

*"Consider the uses of adversity"*

4

chapter IV: WHY BOTHER?

Many people who live in the mountains enjoy extremely active lifestyles and don't want to have a 'hobby' like gardening and yard work consume all their weekends and free time. Most of you, though, appreciate a nice yard, the smell of fresh cut grass, and flowers from the garden arranged in a vase. . .

Your yard does not have to be high maintenance. A few selected yard days throughout the growing season can be satisfying. Planting, pruning, fertilizing, and enjoying an outdoor living space is an integral tradition of growing up. Families need to spend quality time together, outside (So do couples and single people!).

Gardening at altitude is challenging, yet it can be rewarding. You will probably lose one out of every ten things you plant in the beginning, but as your outdoor living space matures, your mortality will go down.

It can be easy to become discouraged but don't. If you learn what to plant, where to place them and how to prepare your soil, it is actually easier to garden at higher altitudes - fewer insects and pests, streamlined plant selection and a shorter gardening-work season. . .

YOU GET TO HAVE THE WINTERS OFF!

NOTES and IDEAS:
*what, when, where, why bother?*

## NOTES and IDEAS:
*what, when, where, why bother?*

*"The difficulty in life is the choice"*
        - George Moore

Favorite Plants:  Plants I (we) definitely want in the yard:

Plants not fond of:

Design ideas I (We) like:

Necessary spaces in the yard:

- Grassy area to play on

- Place for the dog to hang out

- Color!

- Bird watching and attracting

- Human grazing - vegetable and fruit growing space

NOTES and IDEAS:
*what, when, where, why bother?*

*"The important thing is not to stop questioning."*

-Albert Einstein

# REFERENCE

# Index of Plants by Common Name to Scientific Name

Annuals see page 68

Perennials, Wildflowers, Groundcovers and Ornamental Grasses

| | |
|---|---|
| Anchusa | *Anchusa* |
| Arrowleaf Balsamroot | *Balsamorhisa* |
| Aster | *Aster* |
| Astilbe | *Astilbe* |
| Baby's Breath | *Gypsophila* |
| Bachelor Button | *Centaurea* |
| Balloon Flower | *Platycodon* |
| Basket of Gold | *Alyssum* |
| Beacon Silver | *Lamium* |
| Bee Balm | *Monarda* |
| Bellflower | *Campanula* |
| Bishop's Weed | *Aegopodium* |
| Black-Eyed Susan | *Rudbeckia* |
| Blanket Flower | *Gaillardia* |
| Bleeding Heart | *Dicentra luxuriant* |
| Old Fashioned Bleeding Heart | *D. spectabilis* |
| White Bleeding Heart | *D. alba* |
| Blue Bells | *Mertensia* |
| Blue Fescue | *Festuca* |
| Blue Flax | *Linum lewisii* |
| Blue Oat Grass | *Avena* |

# Index of Plants by Common Name to Scientific Name

# Index of Plants by Common Name to Scientific Name

# Index of Plants by Common Name to Scientific Name

| | |
|---|---|
| Iris | *Iris* |
| German | *I. germanica* |
| Siberian | *I.sibirica* |
| Variegated | *I. pallida* |
| Jacob's Ladder | *Polemonium caeruleum* |
| Jupiter's Beard | *Centranthus ruber* |
| Keys to Heaven | *Centranthus ruber* |
| Kinnikinnick | *Arctostaphylos uva-ursi* |
| Lady's Mantle | *Alchemilla erythropoda* |
| Lamb's Ear | *Stachys byzantina* |
| Larkspur | *Delphinium* |
| Lavender | *Lavendula* |
| Lenten Rose | *Helleborus* |
| Leopard's Bane | *Doronicum* |
| Lily | *Lilium* |
| Lily of the Valley | *Pieris japonica* |
| Loveliness | *Prunella* |
| Lungwort | *Pulmonaria* |
| Lupine | *Lupinus* |
| Lymegrass | *Elymus glaucus* |
| Maiden Pinks | *Dianthus deltoides* |
| Maltese Cross | *Lychnis* |
| Marguerite Daisy | *Anthemis tinctoria* |
| Meadow Rue | *Thalictrum aquilegifolium* |
| Meadowsweet | *Filipendula* |
| Mexican Hat | *Ratibida* |
| Mexican Primrose | *Oenothera* |
| Monkshood | *Aconitum cammarum* |
| Mountain Bluet | *Centaurea montana blue* |
| Moss | *Sagina* |
| Mum | *Chrysanthemum* |

# Index of Plants by Common Name to Scientific Name

# Index of Plants by Common Name to Scientific Name

# Index of Plants by Common Name to Scientific Name

TREES:

| | |
|---|---|
| Apple | *Malus* |
| Ash | *Fraxinus* |
| Alder | *Alnus* |
| American Mountain Ash | *Sorbus Americana* |
| Amur Maple | *Acer ginnala* |
| Aspen | *Populus* |
| Austrian Pine | *Pinus nigra* |
| Birch | *Betula* |
| Box Elder | *Acer negundo* |
| Bristlecone Pine | *Pinus aristata* |
| Canada Redcherry | *Prunus virginiana 'Schubertii'* |
| Chokecherry | *Prunus virginiana* |
| Colorado Spruce 'Blue' | *Picea pungens 'glauca'* |
| Cottonwood | *Populus* |
| Lanceleaf Cottonwood | *P. acuminata* |
| Narrowleaf Cottonwood | *P. angustifolia* |
| Crabapple, Flowering | *Malus* |
| Douglas Fir | *Pseudotsuga* |
| European Mountain Ash | *Sorbus aucuparia* |
| Fir | *Abies* |
| Golden Willow | *Salix alba vitellina* |
| Honeylocust | *Gleditsia* |
| Iseli's Fastigit Spruce | *Picea pungens fastigiata* |
| Laurel Leaf Willow | *Salix pentandra* |
| Lodgepole Pine | *Pinus contorta latifolia* |

# Index of Plants by Common Name to Scientific Name

## SHRUBS:

# Index of Plants by Common Name to Scientific Name

| | |
|---|---|
| Cotoneaster | *Cotoneaster* |
| Mountain Mahogany | *Cercocarpus* |
| Currant | *Ribes* |
| Dogwood | *Cornus* |
| Dwarf Mountain Lover | *Pachistima* |
| Dwarf Scotch Pine | *Pinus sylvestris glauca* |
| Elderberry | *Sambucus* |
| Flowering almond | *Prunus glandulosa* |
| Globosa Spruce | *Picea pungens giaucea 'Globosa'* |
| Gooseberry | *Ribes* |
| Honeysuckle | *Lonicera* |
| Juniper | *Juniperus* |
| Kinnikinnick | *Arctostaphylus* |
| Lilac | *Syringa* |
| Mountain Alder | *Alnus tenufolia* |
| Mugo Pine | *Pinus mugo mugus* |
| Nanking Cherry | *Prunus tomentosa* |
| Ninebark | *Physocarpus* |
| Nest Spruce | *Picea abies 'Nidiformis'* |
| Oak | *Quercus* |
| Peking Cotoneaster | *Cotoneaster acutifolia* |
| Potentilla | *Potentilla* |
| Pygmy Pea Shrub | *Caragana* |
| Raspberry | *Raspberry* |
| Rose | *Rosa* |
| Rhubarb | *Rhubarb* |
| Rubber Rabbitbrush | *Chrysothamnus nauseosus* |
| Schubert Chokecherry | *Prunus virginiana 'Schubertii'* |
| Scrub Oak | *Quercus gambelii* |
| Shrubby Cinquefoil | *Potentilla* |
| Serviceberry | *Amelanchier alnifolia* |
| Siberian Peashrub | *Caragana arborescens* |
| Snowberry | *Symphoricarpos albus* |
| Spirea | *Spirea* |
| Sumac | *Rhus* |
| Viburnum | *Viburnum* |
| Western Sandcherry | *Prunus besseyi* |

# Scientific to Common Name Index for Trees:

| | |
|---|---|
| *Abies concolor* | Concolor Fir |
| *Abies lasiocarpa* | Alpine Fir |
| *Acer* | Maple |
| *Acer Freemani* | Autumn Blaze |
| *Acer ginnala* | Amur Maple |
| *Acer negundo* | Box Elder |
| *Alnus* | Alder |
| *Betula* | Birch |
| *Fraxinus* | Ash |
| *Fraxinus Mandchurian* | Mancana Ash |
| *Gleditsia* | Honeylocust |
| *Malus* | Crabapple |
| *Picea* | Spruce |
| *Pinus* | Pine |
| *Populus* | Aspen |
| *Populus* | Cottonwood |
| *Prunus* | Plum, Cherry, Chokecherry |
| *Pseudotsuga* | Douglas Fir |
| *Quercus* | Oak |
| *Rhus* | Sumac |
| *Salix* | Willow |
| *Sorbus* | Ash |
| *Syringa* | Lilac |

## SCIENTIFIC TO COMMON NAME INDEX FOR SHRUBS:

| | |
|---|---|
| *Alnus* | Alder |
| *Amelanchier* | Serviceberry |
| *Arctostaphylus* | Kinnikinnick |
| *Arnonia* | Chokeberry |
| *Artemisia* | Sage |
| *Berberis* | Barberry |
| *Caragana* | Peashrub |
| *Cercocarpus* | Mahogany |
| *Chrysothamnus* | Rabbitbrush |
| *Cornus* | Dogwood |
| *Cotoneaster* | Cotoneaster |
| *Cytisus* | Broom |
| *Euonymous* | Burning Bush |
| *Juniperus* | Juniper |
| *Lonicera* | Honeysuckle |
| *Mahonia* | Oregon Grape |
| *Pachistima* | Dwarf Mountain Lover |
| *Physocarpus* | Ninebark |
| *Picea* | Spruce |
| *Pinus* | Pine |
| *Potentilla* | Potentilla |
| *Prunus* | Chokecherry, Plum, Cherry |
| *Quercus* | Oak |
| *Rhus* | Sumac |
| *Ribes* | Current |
| *Rosa* | Rose |
| *Salix* | Willow |
| *Sambucus* | Elderberry |
| *Shepherdia* | Buffaloberry |
| *Sorbaria* | Ashleaf Spirea |
| *Spirea* | Spirea |
| *Symphoricarpos alba* | Snowberry |
| *Syringa* | Lilac |
| *Viburnum* | Viburnum |

# PRODUCT INFORMATION:

Items listed in "the book" which are registered or have trademarks

ferti*lome® Soil Acidifier plus Iron
Soil Pep®
Ranui Live Compost®
Round-Up®
Killzall®
Morgro® Rootstarter
ferti*lome® Blooming and Rooting
Morgro® Sod & Seed Starter
Park City Nursery's 'Original' Custom Wildflower Blends®
Sevin®
Thiodan®
Daconil®
ferti*lome® Winterizer
Thiram®
Hi-Yield® Terrachlor®
Milorganite®
Poast®
Over-the-top®
Morgro® "Weed it II" with Trimec®
Treflan®
Triamine®
Caseron®
Thuricide®
Ro-Pel®
This-1-Works®
Deer Away®
Felco®
Hi-Yield® Spreader Sticker
Wilt-pruf®

HELPFUL REFERENCE BOOKS FOR HIGH ALTITUDE GARDENING:

A Pictorial Guide to Perennials by M. Jane Coleman Helmer; Karla S. Decker Hodge 1996; Merchant's Publishing company; excellent photos and descriptions of hardy perennials; most of the varieties can survive above 6000'.

Sunset Western Garden Book by the Editors of Sunset Books and Sunset Magazine; 1997; useful descriptions and very complete plant lists; watch the zones – they don't always consider our elevation factors.

Woody Ornamentals for the Prarie by Hugh Knowles; 1995 University of Alberta; excellent descriptions and photos of cold-hardy trees and shrubs.

Popular Series books by Southwest Parks and Monuments Association; series about shrubs and trees of the southwest uplands and others.

# PLANTS IN EXPERIMENTAL STAGES:

One group of people cannot possibly know everything about everything. We are constantly learning about new things related to high altitude gardening. We are *only* interested in plants that THRIVE!

Share with us some of your experiences. We need you to share certain facts with us in order to validate your experiment.

1) Botanical as well as Common name of species - to clarify.
2) How long it has been in the ground?
3) What type of winter and spring has it experienced? Harsh, mild, heavy snow fall, windy, dry, wet. . .
4) What exposure do you have it planted in? Protected, exposed. . .
5) Where (what elevation) you live?
6) What kind of care has the plant received? Ignored, pampered. . .

Some items we are particularly interested in are:

- Climbing Roses
- Vines
- Blueberries
- Pears
- Plums
- Other fruit trees that actually make fruit - in our lifetime.
- Deer, Moose, Elk, Porcupine and Vole Patrol

Write to us at www.parkcitynursery.com OR   Park City Nursery
P.O. Box 631
Park City, Utah 84060